Building Websites with TYPO3

A practical guide to getting your TYPO3 website up and running fast

Michael Peacock

BIRMINGHAM - MUMBAI

Building Websites with TYPO3

A practical guide to getting your TYPO3 website up and running fast

First published: March 2007

Production Reference: 1070307

Published by Packt Publishing Ltd.
32 Lincoln Road
Olton
Birmingham, B27 6PA, UK.

ISBN 978-1-847191-11-3

www.packtpub.com

Cover Image by www.visionwt.com

Credits

Author

Michael Peacock

Reviewer

Ingo Renner

Development Editor

Douglas Paterson

Assistant Development Editor

Nikhil Bangera

Technical Editors

Ajay S

Ved Prakash Jha

Editorial Manager

Dipali Chittar

Project Manager

Patricia Weir

Project Coordinator

Abhijeet Deobhakta

Indexer

Bhushan Pangaonkar

Proofreader

Chris Smith

Layouts and Illustrations

Shantanu Zagade

Cover Designer

Shantanu Zagade

About the Author

Michael Peacock has been building websites since the year 2000. Starting off building websites for friends and family as a hobby, he set up his own business, Think Systems Internet (http://www.thinksystemsinternet.com), in early 2006. Michael is currently in his second year at Durham University studying Computer Science and, while not developing websites or studying, he enjoys taking part in amateur dramatics. Helping customers realize their visions and creating web applications that become integral to their business are just some of the reasons Michael loves being a part of the web development industry.

I would like to thank everyone who has helped make this book possible, in particular Douglas Paterson for introducing me to the world of TYPO3, Patricia Weir, and Abhijeet Deobhakta for keeping me on track, Ved Jha, Ajay S, and Nikhil Bangera for helping me improve and refine this book, Ingo Renner the technical reviewer for ensuring everything was as accurate as possible and of course everybody in the Packt team.

I would also like to thank you, the reader, I hope you enjoy this book—so that all of my efforts have paid off.

I"d like to dedicate this book to my girlfriend Emma, for being there for me and supporting me during the writing of this book.

About the Reviewer

Ingo Renner lives near Frankfurt and started using TYPO3 in 2003. Since then, he has published several TYPO3 extensions and among them TIMTAB is probably his best known. Other than that, he is a member of TYPO3's content rendering group, maintainer of `tt_address`, and kickstarter and co-developer of `tt_news`. Since February 2007, he has also been a core developer. Ingo Renner does freelance work and can be contacted through `www.ingo-renner.com`.

Table of Contents

Preface

Free, open-source, flexible, and scalable, TYPO3 is one of the most powerful PHP content management systems. This book is a fast-paced tutorial to creating a website using TYPO3. If you have never used TYPO3, or even any web content management system before, then you need not look further than this book as it walks you through each step to create your own TYPO3 site. From installation, to initial set up and content entry, and on to customization and adding plug-ins, this book will get you a stable and working TYPO3-based website fast.

What This Book Covers

Chapter 1 introduces content management systems and TYPO3, along with an overview of the TYPO3 community. You will also learn about the sample site that will be developed during the course of this book.

Chapter 2 covers setup and installation of TYPO3. We look at the installers bundled with TYPO3, and tweak the settings of TYPO3 using the install tool.

In *Chapter 3* we explore the many features within the TYPO3 back end. We learn how to create and manage pages and their content, how to use the Rich Text Editor, and why we need templates to make our pages work. Additionally, you will understand the features of the Task Center by using the TYPO3 Extension Manager.

In *Chapter 4* we apply our knowledge of the TYPO3 administration features to create our website. This chapter shows you how pages fit together, how to display content, and how to customize the design. By the end of this chapter you will know how to manage different versions of your website content.

Chapter 5 explores the features available in the TYPO3 front end, in particular the front-end editing features. You will see how these features work, what they do, and how you can edit and create content for our website directly from the website, without needing to navigate through the back end.

In *Chapter 6* we explore TYPO3's user management features. You will set up specific user groups and create users to work on your site's content.

Chapter 7 takes a look at the types of tasks that you must perform regularly to manage your TYPO3 site. It walks you through backing up your site and restoring it whenever needed. We also cover the powerful Workflow and Workspace features and learn how they can be useful to us for collaboration.

In *Chapter 8* we look at the TYPO3 extension manager, and install four extensions, set them up, and link them to our site. We extend our site by adding extensions to rate pages on our site, and one that allows the administrator to look up the hit statistics of his or her site. The message board and shop system extensions let you monetize your TYPO3 site by adding in ecommerce functionalities.

What You Need for This Book

You will need to have a system with a modern CPU running at least 1 GHz, and at least 256 MB of RAM (although more is recommended). You will need a web server application such as Apache or IIS, a database such as MySQL (there are many different databases supported by TYPO3's Database Abstraction Layer, but MySQL is natively supported and is the most stable), and PHP version 4 or above.

Also, you will need ImageMagick (or GraphicsMagick) and GDLib / FreeType, to utilize TYPO3's image manipulation capabilities, and the zlib compression library.

Conventions

In this book, you will find a number of styles of text that distinguish between different kinds of information. Here are some examples of these styles, and an explanation of their meaning.

There are two styles for code. Code words in text are shown as follows: "If we click on the `publish_dir` setting, a variable dialog appears with the correct structure for the setting."

Any command-line input and output is written as follows:

```
cd /home/michaelp/public_html/
```

New terms and **important words** are introduced in a bold-type font. Words that you see on the screen, in menus or dialog boxes for example, appear in our text like this: "clicking the **Next** button moves you to the next screen".

Warnings or important notes appear in a box like this.

 Tips and tricks appear like this.

Reader Feedback

Feedback from our readers is always welcome. Let us know what you think about this book, what you liked or may have disliked. Reader feedback is important for us to develop titles that you really get the most out of.

To send us general feedback, simply drop an email to feedback@packtpub.com, making sure to mention the book title in the subject of your message.

If there is a book that you need and would like to see us publish, please send us a note in the **SUGGEST A TITLE** form on www.packtpub.com or email suggest@packtpub.com.

If there is a topic that you have expertise in and you are interested in either writing or contributing to a book, see our author guide on www.packtpub.com/authors.

Customer Support

Now that you are the proud owner of a Packt book, we have a number of things to help you to get the most from your purchase.

Downloading the Example Code for the Book

Visit http://www.packtpub.com/support, and select this book from the list of titles to download any example code or extra resources for this book. The files available for download will then be displayed.

The downloadable files contain instructions on how to use them.

Errata

Although we have taken every care to ensure the accuracy of our contents, mistakes do happen. If you find a mistake in one of our books—maybe a mistake in text or code—we would be grateful if you would report this to us. By doing this you can save other readers from frustration, and help to improve subsequent versions of this book. If you find any errata, report them by visiting http://www.packtpub.com/support, selecting your book, clicking on the **Submit Errata** link, and entering the details of your errata. Once your errata are verified, your submission will be accepted and the errata added to the list of existing errata. The existing errata can be viewed by selecting your title from http://www.packtpub.com/support.

Questions

You can contact us at questions@packtpub.com if you are having a problem with some aspect of the book, and we will do our best to address it.

1
Introduction

Welcome to *Building Websites with TYPO3!* In the course of this book we are going to take a look at TYPO3 and use it to build and manage a website. We will install the software, get an overview of its back-end features, set up our website, look at the front-end features, manage our website and its users, and also expand our website and its features with extensions.

In this chapter we will learn:

- What a CMS is
- What TYPO3 is
- What TYPO3 can do for us
- What some of its features are
- What other resources are available to TYPO3 users

What is a CMS?

A Content Management System (CMS) is a system that allows users to collaborate to create and manage content for their website. These systems can range from applications installed on your computer—which link into your website to allow you to manage it—to web-based applications, which run on your web server and allow all aspects of the website to be managed directly from the website.

Content management systems are one of the common methods for creating and managing content on the Internet and on intranets, especially in environments where there is more than one person working on the content, or where there is a lot of content involved.

These systems generally give users the ability to:

- Create content
- Manage content
- Manage, provide, and restrict access to content and also the editing of content
- Modify a design layer independent of the site's content
- Collaborate effectively
- Manage versions of content

With a CMS, content and design are kept separate, which means that the design of a website can completely change and it will have no impact on the content of the website. This is quite an important feature as it means that the design need only be changed once, and not across each page of the website. This makes it easy for websites of any size to easily and quickly change their design. Also, it protects the design, as content editors do not need to integrate design into their content, which could cause problems, for instance if the content editors do not know HTML.

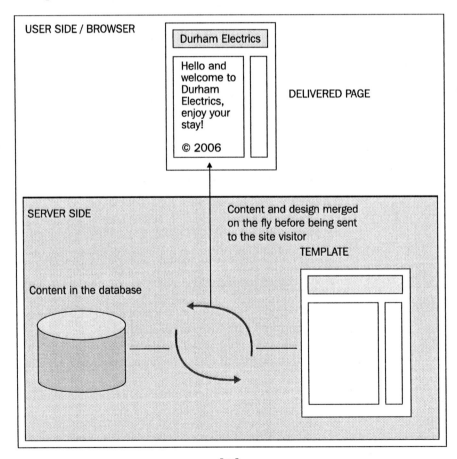

What is TYPO3?

TYPO3 is a free, open-source, enterprise-level content management system originally created by Kasper Skårhøj (a developer from Denmark) in 2000. It is a web-based application that we can run on a web server of our choice. The features that make up TYPO3 are modularized, separating all of the main sections and functions.

TYPO3's License

TYPO3 is released under the **GNU** (General Public License). This means that:

- We are free to modify the source code of TYPO3 for whatever purpose we need.
- We save money on software, and so we can focus on customization.
- It is open source, so security vulnerabilities are more likely to be spotted and quickly patched.

The down side to the license is that the software comes with no warranty. Full details on the license can be found here: `http://www.fsf.org/licensing/licenses/gpl.html`.

What can TYPO3 Do for Us?

With TYPO3 we can quickly and easily create and manage our website's content. New sections can be quickly added and changed easily. Different people can have permissions to edit different sections thereby improving productivity and enhancing collaboration in an easy-to-use web-based environment.

We can control what other back-end users can and cannot access, so that content editors only get access to the content editing tools, and they can use these tools only on the content sections they are allowed to edit. Content changes are versioned, so we can see what changes have been made, and revert to a previous version if necessary.

We can have draft versions of pages, so we could work on improving a page or amending details, and have the content ready for when it needs to be live on the website (when it can be snapped in to replace the existing content at the click of a button). In addition to different versions of content, TYPO3 also allows us to manage different translations of content, providing our visitors with a seamless multilingual site (provided we have editors who can translate our content of course!).

TYPO3 can let us quickly add whole new features to our website using extensions through an interface known as the **extension manager**. This allows us to add features such as guest books, support forums, or voting polls at the click of a button, without needing to install and manage another software application.

Content can be managed easily through familiar-looking rich-text editors and TYPO3's intuitive user interface.

We can even manage multiple websites and domains through the same TYPO3 installation. This is very useful if we have a small business site with different domains for different products or services.

If we are trying to edit the same section or content that someone else is editing, TYPO3 warns us of this and prevents us overriding content that has not yet been submitted.

All of this can be going on while visitors are still viewing the website!

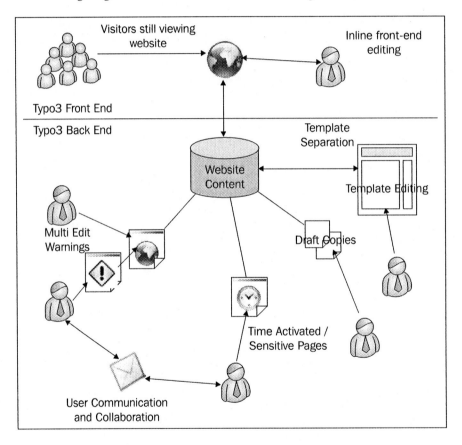

Overview of TYPO3 Features

TYPO3 has a huge list of features—too many to fully list here; the full list can be found on the TYPO3 website `http://typo3.com/Feature_list.1243.0.html`.

Content and Its Management

Naturally with TYPO3 being a content management system, this is where most of its features lie:

- Create, edit, and manage web pages
- Create, edit, and manage individual content items
- A clipboard to copy pages and elements to, in order to paste into different sections later
- Versioning to control changes, and multiple changes
- Workspace and drafts, to create drafts of pages that don't take effect until ready
- Time-controlled pages and content, i.e. content and pages that are only active between a start date and an end date

Users

Our content can be managed by many people; so TYPO3 also has user management features:

- Create, edit, and modify users and their details
- User permissions that control which sections users can and cannot access
- Control over which sections a user can edit and control

Extensions

To expand on the default TYPO3 installation, we have an extension manager, which allows us to:

- Install new extensions to add new functionality
- Remove extensions
- Modify some basic elements of extensions

TYPO3 Resources

TYPO3 is a very community-built system. There are a great number of resources available to help us, and also, to expand and enhance TYPO3.

Getting Help

The typo3.org website is the main resource for TYPO3 users. On this site we have:

- Mailing Lists
- Mailing List Archives
- The facility to ask developers directly
- IRC chat
- Documentation
- Bug reports
- Videos

Documentation and Videos

The documentation section of the typo3.org website, http://typo3.org/documentation/, contains a huge amount of documentation; there are guides to installing, getting started, templates, and **TypoScript**.

There is also a large number of videos available, mostly created by Kasper, showing how to use many of the features of TYPO3: http://typo3.org/documentation/videos/wmv-format/. These videos are a little old, and in some cases may be using slightly older versions of the software, but they are still useful in most cases.

Mailing Lists and Archives

This is an incredibly useful resource on the website. The mailing list archives, http://lists.netfielders.de/pipermail/typo3-english, are full of requests, questions and support that have already been responded to. If the archives don't have what you're looking for, then there are the active lists. There is a list for almost every possible aspect of TYPO3, from a community snowboarding tour to extension development, or just the English users' mailing list. The lists are available at http://lists.netfielders.de/pipermail/typo3-english.

Bug Reports

Occasionally, a feature not working as you expected could be a bug. Searching the bug reports may prove useful in confirming if something is in fact a bug, or so that you can submit the bug to the developers.

Extensions

TYPO3 is very extensible. Huge features and capabilities can be added at the click of a button. These extensions are created by the TYPO3 community members and are mostly accessible through the internal extension manager of TYPO3 itself. All extensions are available on the extension page, `http://typo3.org/extensions/`, and documentation for individual extensions is available with the extension itself.

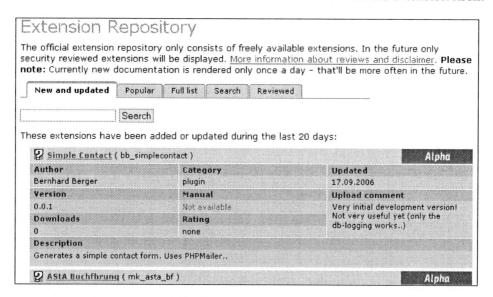

Extensions have a varying degree of stability. Some extensions are completely stable and safe to use while others have not been completely tested and may contain bugs, such as alpha and beta versions of extensions.

There is also documentation on the website for creating extensions, along with coding guidelines and naming conventions.

Sponsorship of Features and Donations

Although TYPO3 is free, it relies heavily on sponsorship and donations. The involvement of Kasper and some of the team depends on if they can afford to focus time on the project. A number of large features, such as the **Database Abstraction Layer**, are commercially sponsored. Companies who wish to use TYPO3 and a particular undeveloped feature fund its development. Since they will be using it in a commercial environment, it seems fair to give something back.

In a similar respect, the TYPO3 community believes that those who use TYPO3 and earn money from such use (such as web developers using TYPO3 to power a client's website) should donate a percentage of their profits to TYPO3.

Our Site

Throughout this book we are going to use our constantly expanding knowledge of TYPO3 to create a website of our own. We will create a point-of-presence (POP) site for a small business. This will allow us to explore a lot of the features within TYPO3 and to expand our site later.

Site Scenario

The website that we are going to develop is for a small fictional electronic goods shop, 'Durham Electrics'. The site will contain the following:

- Basic information about the business
- Contact details and an online contact form
- Search facilities
- List of products and services
- A dedicated area for customers, with some generic information for customers and support information

Because the shop stocks a large range of products the owners have divided their products and services into sections.

An *AV* section specializing in MP3 players, stereos, televisions, etc.; a *computer* section specializing in computers, software, and accessories; and a *services* section, providing in-store repairs and service agreements with products sold.

Each section has a manager who will need to be able to access, edit, and manage his or her own section's content. Trainee staff members will need to be able to edit content only in their appropriate sections (but they will be able to edit only draft versions), and their changes will need to be approved by the section manager.

These are all things that TYPO3 can manage easily. We may decide later to expand on our customer area by adding extensions to provide more interactive sections such as a discussion forum for customers or customer support or a poll system to suggest improvements for the business.

Summary

In this chapter, we have looked at what a CMS is, what TYPO3 is, and how it can help us. We also saw that typo3.org really has all of the resources we could ever need.

We have decided on a project site to create during the course of this book to help us apply our ever growing knowledge of TYPO3. Now it's time to install TYPO3 for ourselves and see what it has to offer in action!

Installing TYPO3

2

Now that we know what TYPO3 is, and what it can do for us, we need to get ourselves a copy and install it.

In this chapter, we will cover:

- Installing a development platform to run TYPO3 (using the **Windows Installer** package, which will also install TYPO3 for us).
- Manually installing the TYPO3 application (using the TYPO3 ZIP file) on a pre-existing development environment (for those with their own development environment setup)
- Configuring TYPO3 using the **Install Tool**.

System Requirements

TYPO3 requires our system to meet some specific requirements.

Hardware

We will need to have a system with a modern CPU running at at least 1 GHz, and at least 256 MB of RAM (although more is recommended). Since we are working (locally) on our own machines, we will also need a keyboard, a mouse, and a screen.

Software

We will need a web server application such as **Apache** or **IIS**, a database such as **MySQL** (there are many different databases supported by TYPO3's **Database Abstraction Layer**, but MySQL is natively supported and is the most stable), and **PHP** version 4 or above.

Also, there are some other optional software applications that are recommended:

ImageMagick (or **GraphicsMagick**) and **GDLib / FreeType**, to utilize TYPO3's image manipulation capabilities, and the **zlib** compression library.

Installing a Development Platform

Depending on the operating system we are using, there are different processes for installing a development platform on our machine. We can either run an **Installer** package that will install Apache, MySQL, and PHP, along with TYPO3 (there are installers available for **Microsoft Windows, Mac OSX**, and **Linux**), or we can install each of these components separately.

> The software included in the installer packages may be out of date. You should periodically check for updates to Apache, PHP, and MySQL to see if there have been further releases that fix any known bugs or security problems.

The Windows Installer Package

The Windows installer will install everything that we need to get started. Firstly, we need to download a copy from the TYPO3 website, `http://typo3.org/download/installers/`. The **Version Target OS** column shows the operating system for each installer. The installer we want is **TYPO3 Winstaller** as, at the time of writing, this installer had the most recent version of TYPO3 and web server software.

Once the file has downloaded, we can double-click on it to initiate the installation process. It is recommended to close all other (open) applications before doing so.

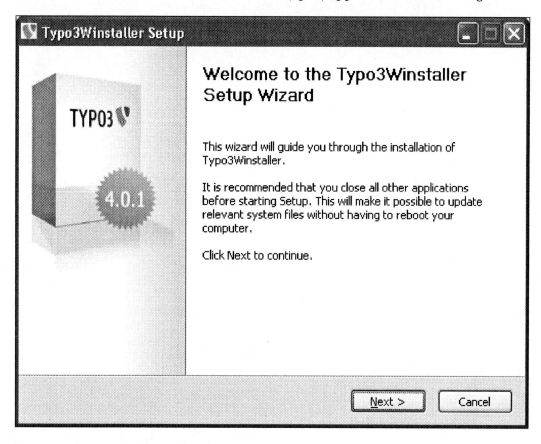

The first stage is just to provide an overview of the installation. After we have read it, we can click on **Next**.

The following screen requires us to accept the GNU (General Public License). This is a license under which the included software programs are released. It must be agreed to, for TYPO3 to be installed. Once we have read and accepted the agreement, we can click on **I Agree**.

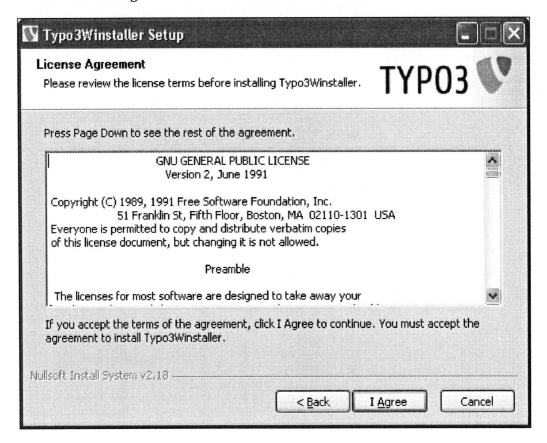

Now that we have accepted the agreement, we can choose the components that we wish to install. We are going to install **TYPO3 4.0.1** (as this includes TYPO3 and all of the other required components). The other two options are just shortcuts and we can choose not to install them if we wish.

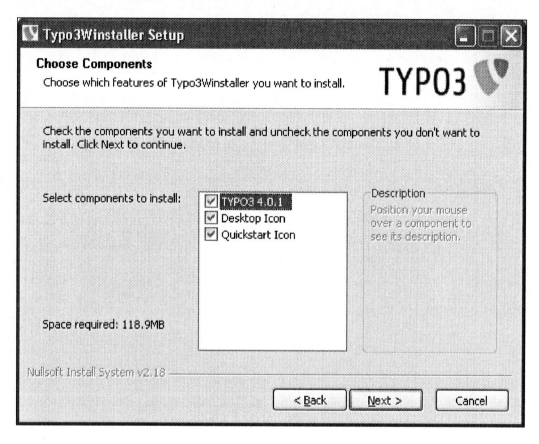

The next stage is to choose the location where TYPO3 is to be installed. The default location is **C:\Program Files\TYPO3_4.0.1**. If we are happy with this location, we can click on **Next**.

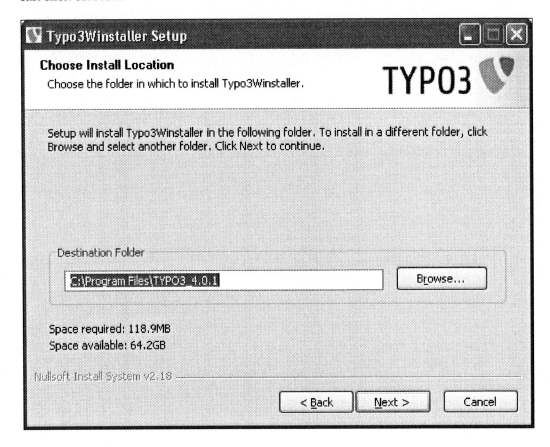

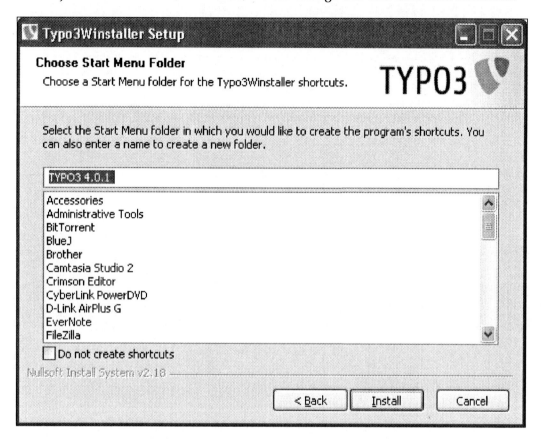

Finally, we can select the folder within the **Start** menu (on the desktop) where we want TYPO3 to be available. The default is **TYPO3 4.0.1**. If we are happy with this, we can just click on **Install**; otherwise, we can change this and then click on **Install**.

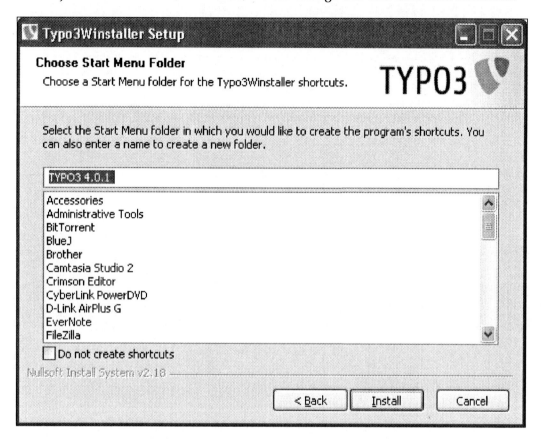

The installer will begin the process of actually installing TYPO3 and the other components needed to run a local web server. This process may take several minutes. Once the installation is complete, there is an option to **Run Typo3Winstaller** and **Show read me** file (once the installer closes).

 Some programs or processes on your computer may be running on port 80. If this is the case, the TYPO3 Winstaller program will fail when trying to start Apache. For instance, some Internet telephony programs such as **Skype**, default to using port 80. You should completely close all such programs when starting the installation, even if they are not visibly running.

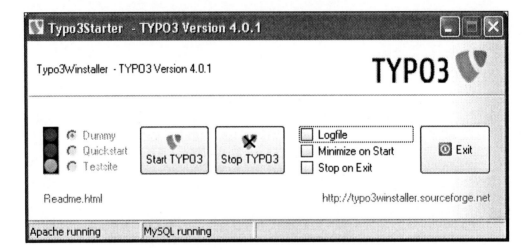

The **Typo3Starter** program that is launched once the installation is complete. This allows us to start and stop our TYPO3 installation, halting both Apache and MySQL, thus allowing us to switch between the three preinstalled TYPO3 packages: **Dummy**, **Quickstart**, and **Testsite**. The **Quickstart** and **Testsite** packages contain demo sites. Later, you may find it useful to try some of these out and see the workings of a pre-built TYPO3 site. The package that we are going to be using is the **Dummy** package. This is because it provides us with a totally blank front end.

Once we click on the **Start TYPO3** button, Apache and MySQL will start and our browser will open a default web page, shown in the following screenshot. This page can also be accessed via http://localhost/.

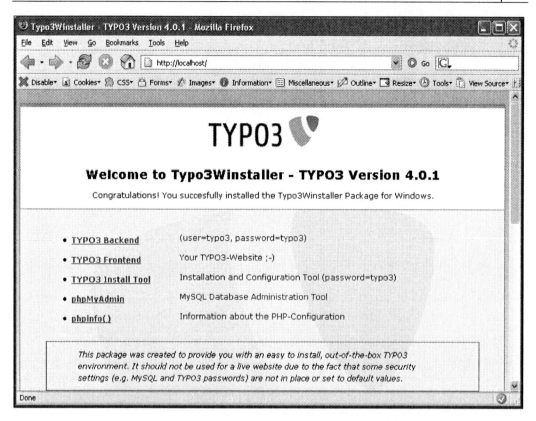

This default page offers us an overview of the access information for our newly installed TYPO3 and **phpMyAdmin** (which is a web-based interface for editing our MySQL database).

If when trying to access TYPO3 you get a blank screen and an error message when accessing phpMyAdmin, this may be a case of files remaining from a previous web server setup. To correct this error you will need to edit the php.ini file (often installed in C:\Windows or C:\Program Files\TYPO3_4.0.2\Apache\bin by the Windows installer package) and modify the extension_dir line to point to the location of your PHP extension folder. Refer to the PHP manual for details.

Manually Installing TYPO3

For those of us with Apache, MySQL, and PHP already installed (or manually installed) we need to manually install TYPO3.

> Depending on the system, there are different processes for installing Apache, PHP, and MySQL manually. With some operating systems, some of these components are automatically installed.
>
> With Linux / Unix-based operating systems, there are often a number of commands available that (when entered in the terminal) will install these applications for us and set them up to work together. It is easiest, however, to use the relevant installer for our particular operating system from the TYPO3 website.

In order to install TYPO3 manually, we need to download two packages from the TYPO3 website, `http://typo3.org/download/packages/`, **TYPO3 Source** and **TYPO3 Dummy**. We need the source package to provide an actual site, and the dummy package has the required files for an empty site (for us to build upon).

Once we have downloaded the two packages, we need to extract the contents of both the files into the same folder (`typo3site`) so as to merge their contents. We can extract the files (using any particular ZIP-handling program such as **WinZip** or **PowerArchiver** or a built-in application) and then move the folder to a location that our local web server can handle. For example: `c:/htdocs/typo3site`.

Now that we have our files in a web-accessible directory, we can install TYPO3!

If we try to load the TYPO3 site folder in our web browser now, we will be redirected to the **Typo3 1-2-3 installer**. So, `http://localhost/typo3site/` will take us to `http://localhost/typo3site/typo3/install/index.php?mode=123&step =1&password=joh316` (which is the 1-2-3 installer) because TYPO3 has not been installed yet.

The first stage of the installer, stage one, asks for our database parameters. We need to enter our username, password, and the hostname (which is usually localhost) of our database server.

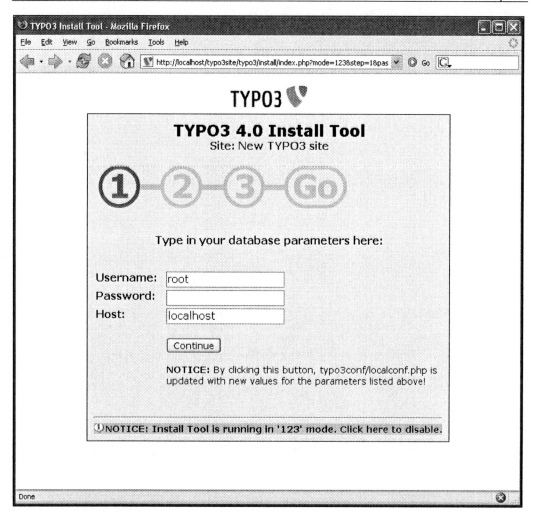

Once we have entered our details, we can click on **Continue** for stage two of the installation process.

The notice at the bottom of the page is just to remind us that we are using the simple 1-2-3 installer. There is a more advanced installation method, which we can access by clicking on the **Click here to disable** link. This link will disable the 1-2-3 installer and take us to the more advanced one. This notice is not something we need to worry about.

Stage two is to set up the database itself. We can either **Select an existing EMPTY database** or enter the name of a new database for the installer to create for us (**Create new database**). The installer recommends that we create a new database using the installer itself, so that is what we will do. Once we have entered the name we want our new database to be called, we click on **Continue**; this is shown in the following screenshot:

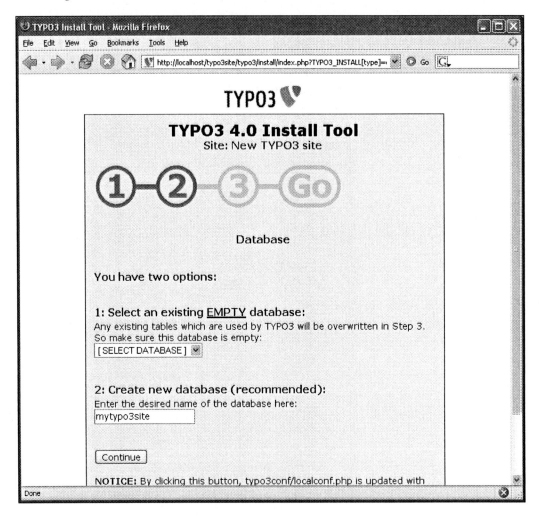

The final step is to tell the installer which database dump we would like to import.

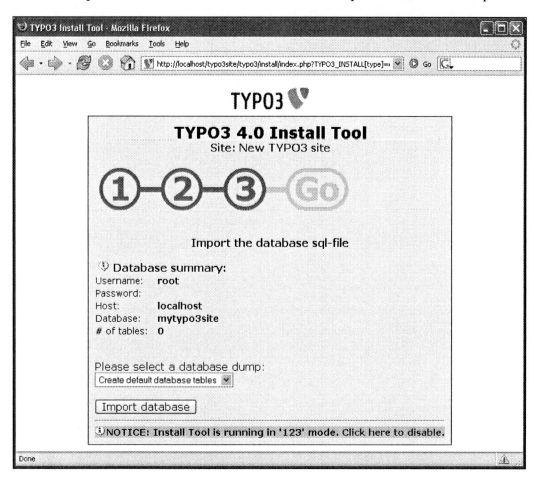

Because we are running a new install through the dummy package, the only option available to us is **Create default database tables**; so we just need to click on **Import database**.

Our TYPO3 installation is now complete! Although the **Install Tool** recommends that we remove the installation directory, change the MD5 Hash that will provide access to it, or password protect it, we should leave it there for the moment to allow us to further configure our TYPO3 installation (once we have completely configured TYPO3, we can remove it). The third link on the **Go** page is to **Continue to configure Typo3**, which utilizes this main install folder. We will cover that next.

Basic Configuration

We can configure our TYPO3 installation by using the main **Install Tool**. There is a default password set on this system, and you maybe asked to enter it when accessing the tool. The default password is *joh316*.

The main **Install Tool** has ten sections of configuration options. Each of these sections is clearly documented within TYPO3.

For security reasons, we should change the **Install Tool** password. The option to do this is under section **10: About**.

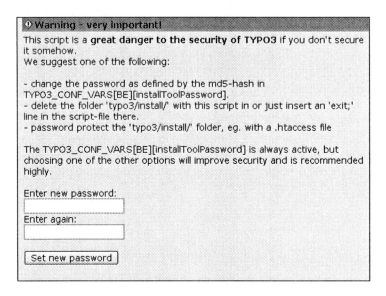

Once we have entered our new password into both boxes and clicked on **Set new password**, we are presented with a screen that tells us that the configuration file has been updated, asking us to **Click to continue**.

This password that we have just set is only for the **Install Tool**. It provides *no* access to the administration function of TYPO3.

Section **5: All Configuration**, lists all of the configuration options available to us. There are a few particular options in here that will be of use to us. At the moment if we were to log in to the TYPO3 back end, our website would be named *New TYPO3 Site* (this and other system variables can be found under the **[SYS]:** heading).

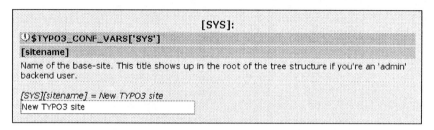

We may also wish to change the date format in this section (as different countries format the date and time differently). The format of the date and time is the same as that defined in the PHP manual (see http://uk2.php.net/date for more information on PHP's date formatting). Personally, I prefer to separate the elements in the date with a '/' as opposed to the default separator of '-'.

Once we have made any changes to this, we need to click on **Write to localconf.php**. We are then asked to **Click to continue** once the changes have been applied.

Another main area that we may like to configure is TYPO3's image processing capabilities.

TYPO3 can utilize both ImageMagick (or GraphicsMagick) and GD2. Although neither is required for TYPO3 to function correctly, they add some enhancements.

The GD2 image library may need to be enabled within PHP itself. To do this, we need to open PHP's ini file (which may be located in c:\Windows\php.ini) and ensure that there is no semicolon before extension=php_gd2.dll.

For ImageMagick, we will need to know the path to ImageMagick (php.ini is located in C:\Program Files\TYPO3_4.0.2\Apache\ bin, **only** if you accepted the default options when installing via the Windows installer package).

We need to configure the graphics options within the **5: All Configuration** option in the **Install Tool**, then we can test the functions in **4: Image Processing** section.

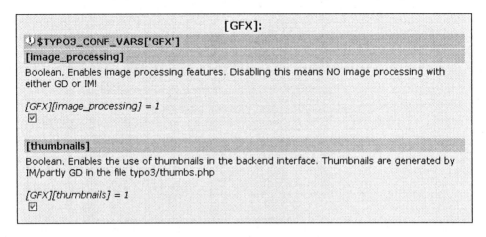

Here, we can enable or disable the image processing capabilities, and also change all of the image processing options. If we have enabled GD within PHP, we can tick the box in here to allow its usage.

GD generally comes with PHP, but needs to be enabled within the `php.ini` file as explained earlier.

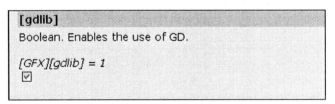

The ImageMagick path is set here too (if we are using a Linux system, this path can be discovered automatically by the **Install Tool**).

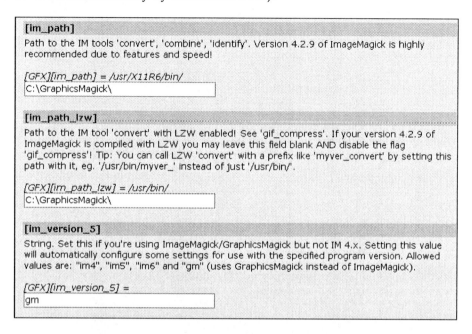

Once we have configured these settings, we can test them in the **4: Image Processing** section of the tool. The reference image is the image included normally through HTML. The first image is an image processed by the server. This could involve including a static image, and applying some special effects to it (or resizing it). If the images are being processed correctly, then the two are identical.

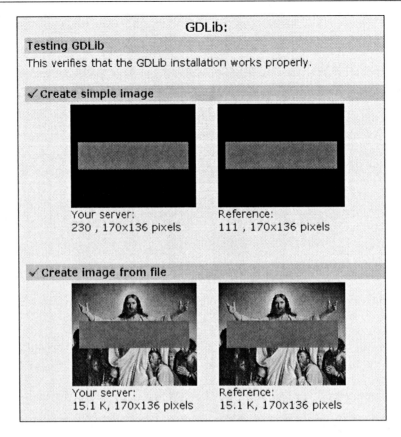

Summary

We have now successfully installed TYPO3! We started with our computer and installed all the components required to install and use TYPO3 on our own systems. We have looked at the bundled installers that TYPO3 provides, and we have looked at changing some of the settings of TYPO3 using the install tool. Also, we have secured the **Install Tool** by changing the default password to one of our own.

We are ready to log in to the system and explore the features it has to offer, and to start creating our very own website powered by TYPO3!

3
Administration Overview

We now have TYPO3 installed on our system, so it's time to look through the TYPO3 back end to see its features and how they work. In this chapter, we will learn:

- How to access and log in to our TYPO3 back end
- How the TYPO3 back end is structured and organized
- What the various modules of TYPO3 are and how to use them

Let's Log In

Firstly, we need to log in to the TYPO3 back end.

The TYPO3 back end is located in the typo3 folder within our main installation. For those of us who used the Windows installer, our back-end login will be situated at http://localhost/typo3/typo3/.

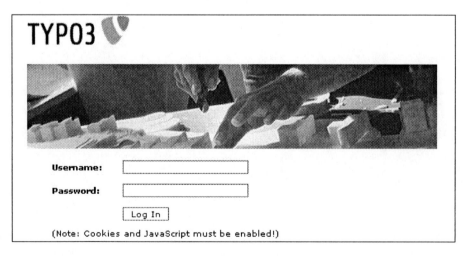

The default username is *typo3*, and the default password is also *typo3*.

If you installed TYPO3 using the **1-2-3 Install** tool, the default username is *admin* and the default password is *password*. Enter those details into their respective boxes and click on **Log In**.

Now that we are logged into TYPO3, we need to familiarize our selves with the back end.

The Back-End Layout

The TYPO3 back end is set out into three main sections:

On the left there is the **Module Bar**, which contains all of the available modules.

In the middle there is the **Navigation Area**, which generally contains a tree structure of the website.

On the right-hand side there is the **Details View**, which is normally where various aspects of pages and settings are changed.

At the bottom of each page, there is a handy **Search Box**, which allows you to search for pages and content, and the **Workspace Switcher**, which allows you to switch between live and draft workspaces.

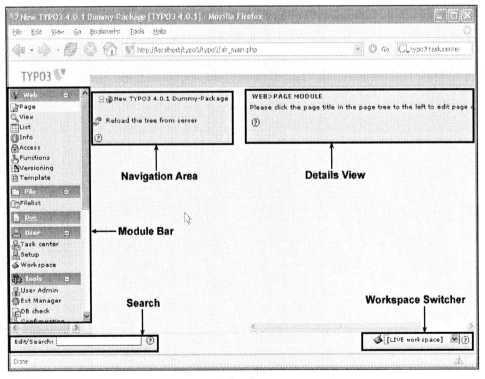

TYPO3 Modules

The main section of the TYPO3 back end is broken-up into modules. A module is a section of the back end that controls a particular aspect of TYPO3.

- We have the **Web** module for working with our website's content. This will be our most frequently used module.

- The **File** module lets us manage files that we use within our website.

- The **Doc** module lets us easily access pages that we have opened and are editing.

- We can view users who access TYPO3 and compare their permissions using the **User** module.

- Tools and settings can be accessed from the **Tools** module.

- The **Help** module gives us quick access to a number of help topics for working with TYPO3.

- The **Admin Functions** module contains some infrequently used maintenance-related tasks.

Web

The **Web** module contains all the tools for creating, maintaining, and managing your website and its content. In the next chapter, we will be exploring this module a lot more to create our website!

Page

With the **Page** sub-module, you can create pages, edit pages, manage versions of the page in different languages, and manage page content. This sub-module is very similar to the **Doc** sub-module mentioned earlier; however, the **Doc** sub-module is intended for files that are currently being edited or that are already opened by a user.

If we click on the world icon next to our site name, a menu appears. This menu allows us to create our first page.

 Clicking on the icons will bring up the menu, and clicking on the text next to the icons will load new content into the details view. The menu does not load immediately because of the JavaScript used to generate it. It may take a few seconds to display.

The **New** button brings up a create **New record** section in the details view:

A new record can be any of the things listed in the screenshot. Because we only want to create a page to help us explore TYPO3's features, we can just click on the **Create a new page** link at the bottom. TYPO3 then wants to know where we want the page to go within its tree structure (this is particularly useful when displaying menus and site maps on our pages).

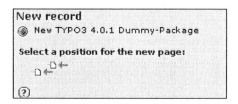

Because we currently have no pages, the root note button will be appropriate; also there are no other pages it could be a sub-page of. Now, we need to give the page a name and then save it by clicking on the **Save** button. Once we have pages within our site, we can then properly access the functions of this sub-module.

The other two options shown are **Hide page** and **Type**. The **Hide page** option is set if the page will be invisible to visitors to the website. The **Type** refers to what the page will be storing. Later, we will look at this in some more detail.

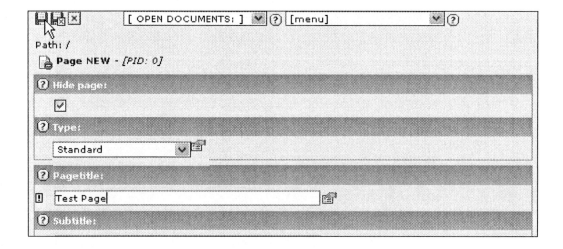

If we click on a page from within the tree, we can then edit the page content.

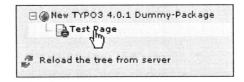

Clicking on the name of the page opens the **Pagecontent** section in the details view. Sometimes when we create pages, the navigation tree may not refresh to reflect the new pages we have added. We can force the tree to refresh by clicking on the **Reload the tree from server** link (shown in the above screenshot).

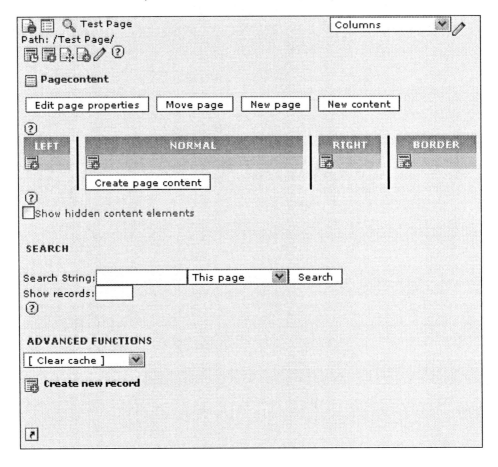

Within this section, we can add various content elements to different sections of the page. We can also use the icons at the top to add content, move the page, set when the page is visible, edit the properties of the page, and create a new page. The TYPO3 back end offers a nice menu for each individual page, providing us with an easy method to edit a page, its settings, and its properties.

If we click on the icon next to the page's name in the navigation area, or if we click on the same corresponding icon when in the detail view, a menu appears (the menu does not load immediately and may take a few seconds to display).

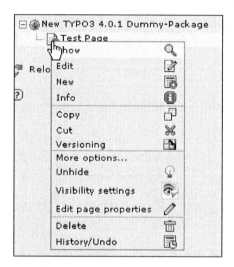

From this menu, we can quickly view the page in a new window, edit the page, create a new page, view its information, cut or copy the page, alter its versioning settings, view more options, change the page's visibility and properties, delete the page, and view its history.

Page Content

Now that we have had an overview of the **Page** sub-module in TYPO3, let us have a look at creating and managing page content in our pages.

Depending on the template used, the page is divided into (up to) four sections: **LEFT,** **NORMAL, RIGHT,** and **BORDER**. We can add different content elements to each of these sections by clicking on the relevant new-record button.

So if we want to add content to the main body of the page, we would add it to the NORMAL section. Then, we would choose which type of page content we wish to add to this section. There are four main types of content:

- Typical page content
- Special Elements
- Form Elements
- Plugins

Typical Page Content

Typical page content is static information that we add to the page such as text, images, tables, bullet lists, or a combination.

Typical page content	
○	**Regular text element** A regular text element with header and bodytext fields.
○	**Text with image** Any number of images wrapped right around a regular text element.
○	**Images only** Any number of images aligned in columns and rows with a caption.
○	**Bullet list** A single bullet list.
○	**Table** A simple table with up to 8 columns.

Just clicking on the radio button next to one of these content types will automatically take us to the appropriate page.

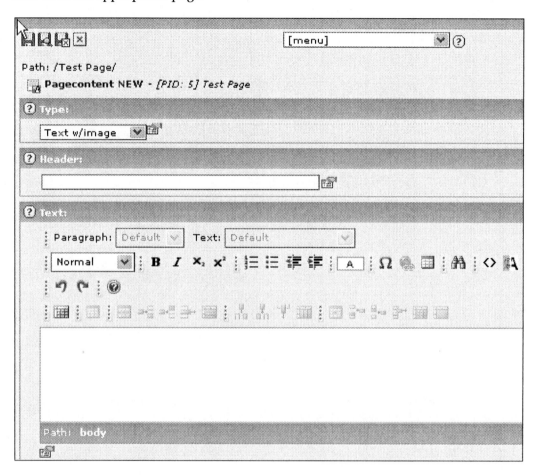

We can easily change the type of content we are adding using the **Type** drop-down menu. Most of the typical page content elements use the same fields, with a few additional fields that are unique to that particular type. The previous picture shows the typical fields. We have the **Type**, which in this case is text with image (**Text w/ image**); we have a **Header** field, which is the heading for this content element; and a **Text** area.

By default the text area utilizes a **Rich Text Editor** that allows us to apply formatting to the text and see the changes it makes on the fly (similar to using a word-processing application). The buttons above the text area provide us with the different formatting features to add to the text. We can add tables, view the content as HTML, remove formatting, undo changes, redo changes, get help, manage tables, insert symbols, and more (using the relevant buttons).

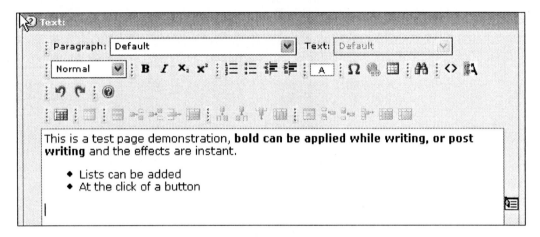

At the top of the page we have the following toolbar:

With this we can, save, save and then view the page, save and then close the editor, close the editor, delete the element, or undo / redo the last change.

Special Elements

Special elements are a little more advanced and dynamic than typical page elements.

Here, we can:

- Have a list of files that our visitors can download
- Add animation and video
- Add an interactive sitemap of the website
- Just add some plain old HTML to our page

Each of these elements is created differently from the others, unlike the typical page elements that were mostly similar to each other.

Form Elements

Many websites allow for some form of user interaction, and out of the box, TYPO3 provides a small number of interactive features.

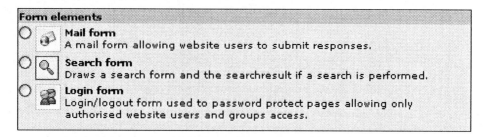

- There is a **Mail form** to allow website visitors to send an email to us using a web-based form.
- We can create a **Search form** so they can search our website.
- We can add a **Login form** for protected pages.

Plugins

There are a number of extensions that when installed add additional features and functionality that can be accessed via the front end by our visitors. These extensions can be added via a plugin.

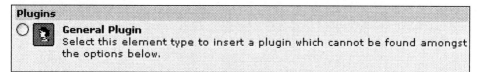

When we create our website, we may decide that we want to add an extra feature, such as *a guestbook* to collect basic feedback from the visitors. We can install this as an extension, which will then provide us with the option to add the guestbook as a plugin.

Managing Content Elements

We can manage the content elements on our web pages in a similar way to managing the pages themselves. We can edit elements, move them around, toggle their individual visibility, delete them, copy them, cut them, and view information on them.

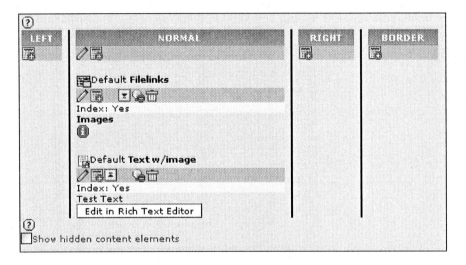

Similarly to the pages themselves, we can click on the elements icon, and a handy menu appears, providing us with quick access to change and manage our content elements.

Other Page Tools

We have had a brief look at some of the features of the **Page** sub-module. Many of the sections of this sub-module contained the same settings and features. Both pages and content elements can be cut, pasted, copied, hidden, and so on. Now we will look into these features.

If we have an element in the main body of the document, and we want to move it to the left or the right-hand side (provided there is already some existing content in the other section), we can cut it from its current location (using the menu available when clicking an element's icon), and paste the element in its new location.

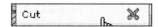

To paste it into a new location, we just need to click on the icon of the element *above* which we want to paste, and click on **Paste after**.

This will then cause a prompt to ask us to confirm if we wish to move the element from its current location to the new selected location. We just need to click on **OK**.

Although when pasting we can only paste below an element, we can then move the element around within its column using the move buttons. With the item we have just moved to a new column, we need to click on the 'move record up' button. The 'move up' and 'move down' buttons are displayed under the content element's name, as shown in the following screenshot:

As well as being able to simply hide or show a particular page or element, we can also change a number of settings relating to its visibility. We can make a page or element appear on a certain date, disappear at a certain date, or hide it based on access. This may be useful for a time-limited offer, or to hide external advertisements from staff or paid customers.

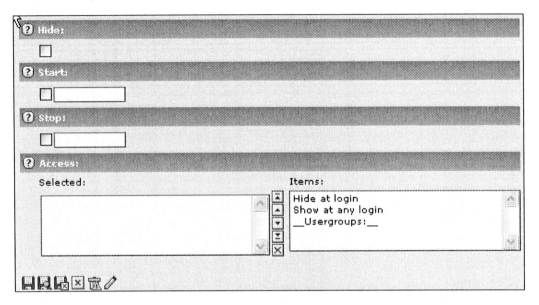

These settings can be accessed via the **Visibility settings** on the menu that is displayed by clicking on the icon of a page or element.

View

The **View** sub-module will allow us to view our pages from within the TYPO3 back end, by opening the page into the details view pane. At present, trying to view any pages that we may have created will result in an error. This is because we do not have a template defined with any of our pages. We will apply a style to our pages in the section *Apply the Style* in the next chapter.

We can either click on the **View** sub-module and then select the page that we wish to view (from the navigation tree), or we can jump from editing the page (in one of the other modules), and click the **View** sub-module link, which will show us the page we were editing or working with. The following image shows how a page would be viewed, but since we do not yet have a template set up for any page, we will get an error message.

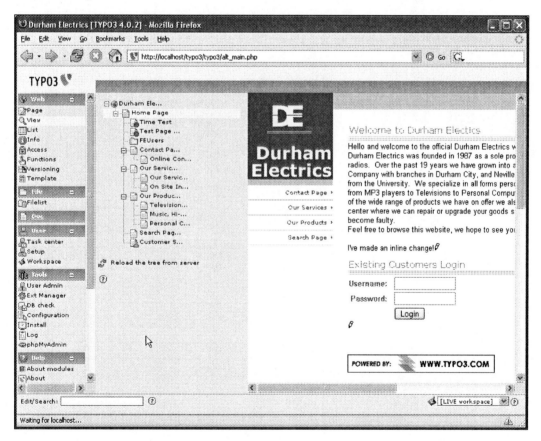

List

The **List** sub-module provides a more advanced view of a page structure and content. Page content is listed down the main section of the page with all of the various page editing tools displayed alongside the content's name. The clipboard is shown on screen with any pages or content elements that we may have copied to be pasted elsewhere, later.

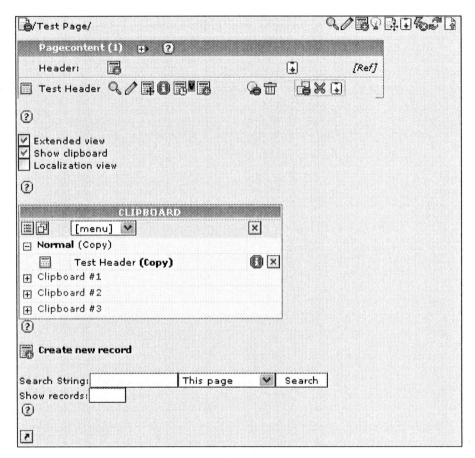

Unlike the **Page** view, this section does not rely as much on the menu that is accessed by clicking an element's icon. This interface is probably something that the more experienced of us will find useful.

Info

With the **Info** sub-module, we can see the history of changes that have been made to a particular page. Additionally, this section can be extended to show page visit and hit statistics by installing appropriate extensions. These different functions can be accessed from the drop-down menu at the top right-hand corner of the page.

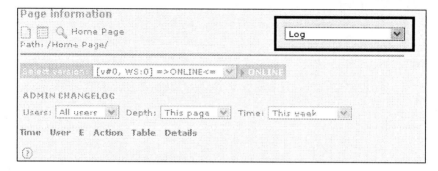

Access

The **Access** sub-module allows us to set editing permissions for a particular page. We may have different users to edit different sections. To ensure that each user can only edit the section or page that he or she is supposed to, this can be enforced with the editing permissions.

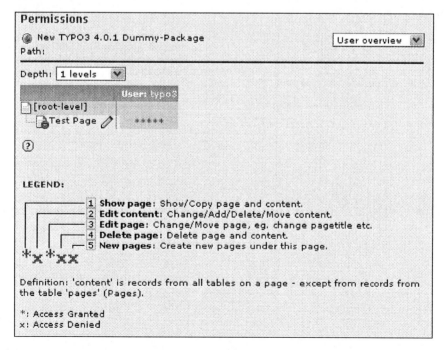

The **User overview** display shows the permissions for our login (i.e. the user whom we are currently logged into the back end). The **Permissions** view shows the permissions for a page's owner, group, and everyone.

With these permissions, either individual users can be assigned a particular permission to edit pages or sections, or particular groups can be assigned these permissions. We will set up some users and permissions and explore this section in more detail in Chapter 6.

Functions

This provides us with some advanced functions in the form of wizards that can make our lives as administrators easier by simplifying some common tasks. Out of the box this includes two wizards:

- **Create multiple pages**
- **Sort pages**

More wizards and functions can be added by installing relevant extensions.

Versioning

With TYPO3 we can have multiple versions of the same page. This could be so that different users could edit different versions, or so that we can revert back to a previous version of a page.

The **Versioning** sub-module only shows information once we have created new versions of a page.

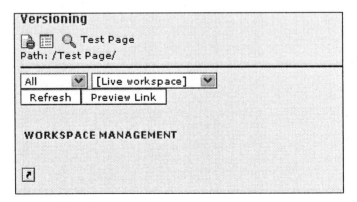

At present, there is little to see in this section as we have no versions enabled. Once we do enable a version for a page, we will see a table of data displayed beneath the **WORKSPACE MANAGEMENT** heading.

To create a new version of a page, we need to use the **Versioning** option from the page menu.

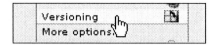

This takes us to the versioning center for that particular page, which at the moment has only one version. We can create a new version of the page by entering a name for the version and clicking on the **Create new version** button at the very bottom of the page.

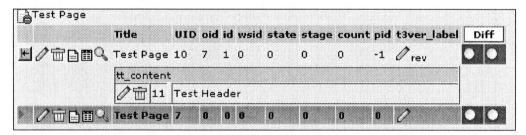

The live version is indicated by the red triangle in the far left box. A version that's not live can be swapped with the live version, by clicking on the button with the arrow on it. We can edit and delete versions in the same way as we manage pages, and we can edit the content of versions in the same interface as is used in the page sub-module. The magnifying glass icon will allow us to view the page or version of the page.

Template

Without templates, our website will not display.

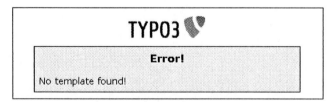

This is because TYPO3 combines the content and structure from the database, along with any special functions, with a template. A TYPO3 template is *a database record containing rendering information and configuration for the page design, menus, content elements, and plugins.* By combining the template with the data, we get a page that can then be rendered by our browser (the concept of templates was illustrated by a figure in Chapter 1).

To apply a template to a page, we can select the page in the navigation tree and click on the **Template** button.

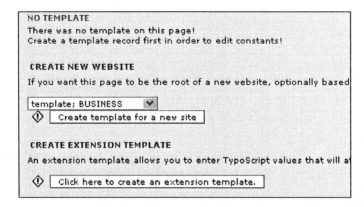

We can select a predefined template from the drop-down list and then click on **Create template for a new site**. This tells TYPO3 to combine this particular template when serving the content for that page.

File

The **Filelist** module provides us with an interface to manage the files used to create a web page in TYPO3. Files that we have uploaded as part of page content are stored in here, and we can use this section to upload files directly to the structure. We can also directly access these files from the fileadmin folder within our TYPO3 installation.

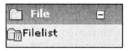

Doc

The **Doc** module stores all open documents in the TYPO3 back end.

These documents are pages and content elements that we have recently selected to edit or manage.

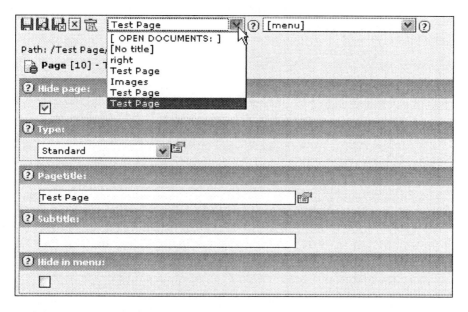

We can quickly switch between documents we are editing using the document selector drop-down menu, and also see which records are still open, preventing other users from editing them.

User

The **User** module lets us communicate with other users via the **Task center** and manage user accounts in the **Setup** section.

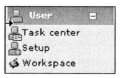

Task Center

The **Task center** module provides an area for users to manage tasks, leave notes for themselves and others, and for other communication.

You may be surprised to find that when you click on the **Task center**, you are presented with a page that appears to do nothing. We need to install some extensions, via the extension manager to add features and functionality to this section.

Later in this chapter we will enable some of these features using the extension manager. The table shown in the screenshot is currently unused. It is linked to the export button shown there, but there is no functionality tied to this button. Once we enable some of the features here by installing some extensions, the empty table of data will be removed and replaced with a **To-Do** list.

Setup

The user **Setup** sub-module is where our users' settings and preferences are. We can change our password, personal details, and personal preferences in this section.

We can specify if we will use the rich text editor, we can have the back end take us straight to the **Task center**, change how the back end is displayed for us, change our password, and then apply the settings by clicking on **Save Configuration**. It is recommended that we update our personal data with our name, email address, enable notification of account logins (for security), and change our password.

If we need to change the settings of another user, we must *simulate* that user, and then change their settings. To do this, we can select their username from the drop-down menu; and we can then edit their settings and preferences.

Simulating the user tells the TYPO3 back end that we are that user, and that we are changing our own settings (and not trying to change the settings of another user). Only admin users can simulate other users.

Workspace

Workspaces allow us to change how we work within TYPO3. We have a **LIVE workspace**, which publishes work in a live format, and we have a **Draft workspace** in which all changes will be made to a new copy of the live content—this is something that can be handled in the **LIVE workspace** using versioning. When using the **LIVE workspace** the workspace manager lists draft documents and their status.

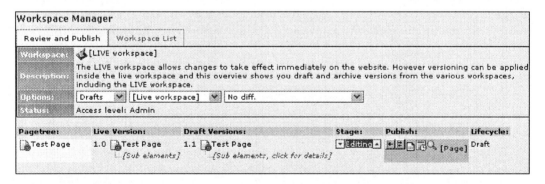

We can also create new workspaces with custom settings to improve our working environment from this section, in the **Workspace List** tab.

Tools

The **Tools** module provides you with a number of useful tools for configuring and enhancing your TYPO3 installation.

User Admin

Users and groups are managed in the **User Admin** sub-module. We can create users, edit users, delete them, compare them, and switch to (or simulate) them here.

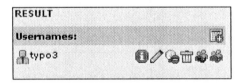

When we create or edit a user, we can choose which areas of the TYPO3 back end they are allowed access to, select which workspaces they can use (preventing some users from making live changes), and select which operations they can perform on files.

Extension Manager

We can extend our TYPO3 installation with TYPO3 extensions. These are often modules (or sub-modules) created by the community for TYPO3 users. There are some extensions that are included with TYPO3 but are not installed, and some are installed as default. For example, the rich text editor (which allows us to format the content of our web pages easily) is an extension that was enabled when we installed TYPO3.

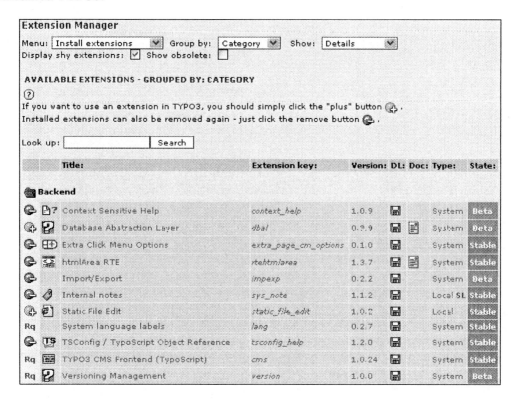

The drop-down menu at the top allows us to select the actions we wish to perform, from viewing all extensions, to changing settings, to just viewing extensions that are already installed.

For us to install a new extension is simply a case of clicking the '+' icon next to the extension's name. It is important for us to note the **State** of any extensions that we wish to install, as **Test** and **Beta** extensions may not function correctly. Some extensions require the database to be changed when we select to install the extension. TYPO3 asks us if we would like to make these changes automatically, and shows us exactly what changes it wants to make. We can easily remove extensions by clicking the '–' button next to them; however extensions with **Rq** next to their name cannot be removed as they are required for TYPO3 to function correctly.

DB Check

This tool allows us to check the integrity of our database, and view how our website is stored within TYPO3 and the database.

Configuration

All of the configurable elements of our TYPO3 installation are stored in here, grouped by their categories, including: graphics, system, extension, back end, etc.

```
$TYPO3_CONF_VARS
  [+] [GFX]
  [-] [SYS]
        [sitename]=New TYPO3 4.0.1 Dummy-Package
        [compat_version]=4.0
        [encryptionKey]=Typo3Winstaller
```

Unfortunately we cannot actually edit the settings directly here. Clicking on a setting will show us a text box containing the full setting string, which we can change, but to actually apply the settings we have to change the value in the configuration file itself.

```
Variable:
$TYPO3_CONF_VARS['SYS']['sitename'] = 'Durham Electrics';
(Now, copy/paste this value into the configuration file where you can set it. This is all you can do from here...)
```

Install

Provided we have left the Install tool intact after we completed our installation of TYPO3, we can still access it from the **Tools** menu, as a convenient way to edit settings without editing the configuration file as the configuration tool requests. We have seen this in Chapter 2.

By default the Install tool is password protected to prevent unauthorised access. The default password for this is: *joh316*.

Log

Each user's actions are logged and we can view them in the **Log** tool. Some of the logs even provide us with the option to view the history of changes made to some files.

```
28-08-06
Time   User        Type    E  Action  Details
11:31  typo3@-99   LOGIN      LOGIN   User typo3 logged in from 127.0.0.1 () (msg#255.1.1)
04:11  typo3@LIVE  [4]        [4_0]   User changed workspace to "0"
04:08  typo3@Draft .          .       User changed workspace to "-1"
03:16  typo3@LIVE  DB         Insert  Record 'NEW SITE, based on standard' (sys_template:6) was inserted on page 'Test Page'
                                      (10) (msg#1.1.10)
02:51  .           .          .       New version created of table 'tt_content', uid '0' (msg#1.1.10)
       .           .          .       New version created of table 'pages', uid '7' (msg#1.1.10)
       .           .          Delete  Record 'Test Page' (pages:9) was deleted from page '[root-level]' (0)
02:50  .           .          .       Record 'Test Header r' (tt_content:10) was deleted from page 'Test Page' (9)
02:49  .           .          Update
                                      Record 'Test Header r' (tt_content:10) was updated. Changes in fields: header.
                                      (msg#1.2.10)
02:47  .           .          .
                                      Record 'Test Header' (tt_content:10) was updated. Changes in fields: bodytext.
                                      (msg#1.2.10)
```

We can view the logs for all users of the system, or a particular user of the system, and even particular types of logs, such as setting changes or logins. The icon of a page with a clock in it allows us to see the history of that particular record.

The feature to view the history of changes seems problematic under Windows. Initially it would take longer than PHP's allowed execution time (which can be changed in the php.ini file, which for Windows users is in the C:\Windows directory). I also found a number of instances of a non-responding task of cmd.exe, but eventually the page loaded. Some issues have been raised regarding this in the TYPO3 bug tracker: http://bugs.typo3.org/view.php?id=1984.

The history of a page is displayed on screen as shown in the following screenshot listing the various versions and history of the page.

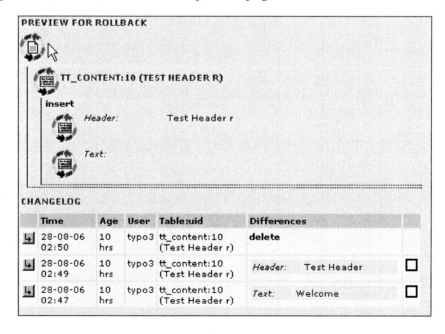

This history allows us to roll back to a particular version or edit of a particular element, or to roll back all changes that have been made.

phpMyAdmin

This is a very useful tool to have when working with PHP and MySQL. It is a web-based interface to manage your MySQL databases, and is installed along with TYPO3 for your convenience.

Help

There is a **Help** module, which contains a number of help features, available in addition to various inline help sections.

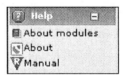

Inline Help

The TYPO3 back end contains a lot of inline help buttons in addition to the main help area (which we will discuss further on in this chapter). If we find a feature or an input box, and we don't understand what it is for or how to use it, we can click on the corresponding help icon next to it.

Many menu items and links have tool tips assigned to them. This means that when we move our mouse cursor over some parts of the TYPO3 back end, a little information box is displayed giving a slightly more descriptive explanation of what that section or button does.

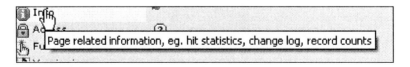

About Modules

This page gives us an overview of all the modules in TYPO3 and explains what each of them is used for.

About

This is TYPO3's about page, with information on TYPO3's license and copyright notices.

Manual

The manual page is an interactive inline help section documenting most of TYPO3's features. Accessing the manual in this way allows us to browse through it or view it as one document. The inline help prompts (which are displayed by clicking the question mark buttons next to features) take the help content from sections of this manual.

Admin Functions

These functions allow us to clear some of TYPO3's cache. Cached content makes it quicker to serve pages, as they are not dynamically generated on the fly. We should only clear these caches when TYPO3 recommends or suggests we do so, as clearing the cache can affect our site's performance for a short while.

The Task Center in Detail

The **Task center** has a lot of capabilities, which surprisingly are not available when we first install TYPO3. These features need to be activated.

Activating the Task Center

We will take a closer look at the extension manager (which we looked at earlier); once in the extension manager, we need to ensure we are in the **Install Extensions** section from the drop-down menu at the top.

Under the **Backend modules** heading we can see a number of extensions related to the **Task center**, which are not installed, and that the center itself is installed.

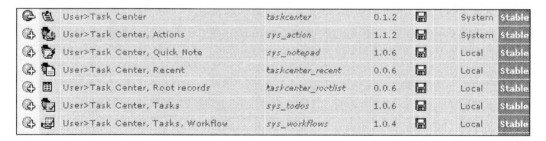

These tools will give additional functionality to the task center; some allow us to record tasks, some allow us to create notes, and some provide other features. We can install these by clicking the '+' icon next to their names.

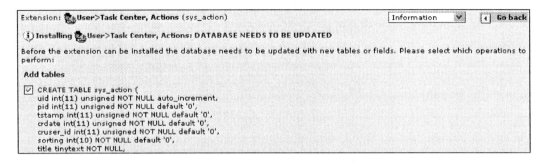

It then asks us to confirm if we wish to make the relevant database changes, so we click on the **Make updates** button to change the database.

The Task Center

Now, when we go to the **Task center** we should see a working module.

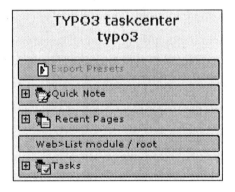

Quick Note

The **Quick Note** feature gives us each a personal notepad area, where we can leave notes for ourselves. We just click on the + button next to quick note, and a pencil icon appears for us to click (although it appears obscured by the menu items below). This opens up a large notepad space for us.

Recent Pages

Any records or pages that we have recently edited are stored under the **Recent Pages**, so we can quickly access pages that we have been working on recently.

List Module / Root

This provides us with an alternative version of the **List** sub-module that was under the **Web** module.

Tasks

Here we can create tasks that need to be completed. The tasks can be intended for any user in the system, and are assigned deadlines, descriptions, and workflows.

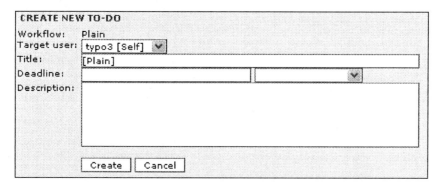

To-Do items are then displayed under the **Tasks** section; once the item has been completed, it is removed from under the **Tasks** heading, and is only available through the **Task** inbox.

Back-End Warnings

Manual Installs

For those of us who installed TYPO3 manually, without the aid of a bundled installer program, we have two extra warning messages waiting for us when we first access the TYPO3 back end.

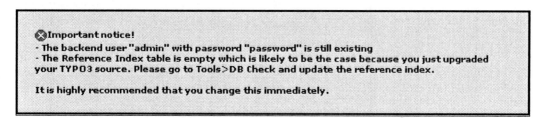

To change our user password, we need to go to the **Setup** section under the **User** module, and under **PERSONAL DATA**, enter a new password twice, and then click on **Save Configuration**. To remove the other warning, we need to go to the **DB check** section under **Tools** and click the option to update the reference index. This is an index of data kept by TYPO3.

All Installs

Unless we have changed the password for the Install tool during the installation process, we will have an error similar to that for those of us with manual installs, telling us that we have the default Install tool password.

We can change this by going to the Install tool under the **Tools** menu, logging in with our default password of *joh316* and changing the password on the first page we are shown.

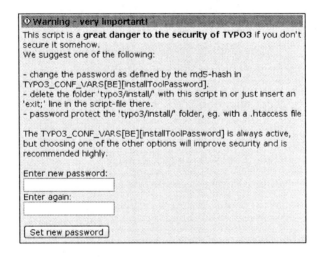

Although those of us using the bundled installers won't have an error message about our password being the default, we should still change our password to be more secure.

Summary

In this chapter we have explored the many features within the TYPO3 back end. We have learned how to create and manage pages and their content, how to use the rich text editor, and why we need templates to make our pages work. Additionally we have enabled some of the features of the **Task center** by using the TYPO3 extension manager and explored the new features that the extension manager has provided us with. Finally we have removed the warning notices from the back end.

4
Setting Up the Site

Now that we know the features and workings of the TYPO3 back end, it's time for us to really start using TYPO3 and set-up our website! In this chapter we will learn:

- How to apply our knowledge from Chapter 3, in order to build a website
- What templates are available to us
- How to customize templates
- Basic uses of content versioning

We will start with our first page, and then take a step back to look, in detail, at the templates available to us, and how to use them. Once we have explored the templates, we will return to creating the rest of our site. After we have built our website, we will return again to the templates, and customize the template we are using, and also look at some of the versioning features.

Our Site

As discussed in Chapter 1, we are going to create a point-of-presence website for a small electronics firm, Durham Electrics.

We said in Chapter 1 that the site will contain the following:

- Basic information on the business
- Contact details and an online contact form
- Search facilities
- A list of products and services
- A dedicated customer-only area with some generic information for customers and support information

Once completed, it will be structured like this:

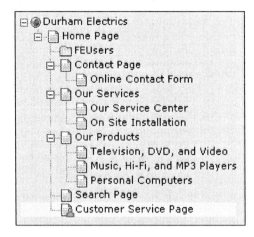

Creating our First Page

Let's start, with the website's homepage. On this page we will add some information about the business, so for now, once we have created the page, we will create a single page content element for the text.

Create the Page

Once we are logged in, we create a new page by clicking on the globe icon (from the page tree in the **Page** section of the **Web** module) and selecting **New** from the menu that pops up.

[Don't forget—sometimes the menu takes a few seconds to appear!]

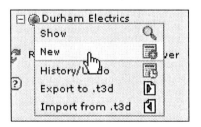

We are then asked which type of record we would like to create, and we of course want to create a new page; so we can click on the **Page (inside)** link.

Obviously we want our page to be visible; so we will uncheck the **Hide page** box. This can be a problem sometimes, as it's the first option, and it's a checkbox. It's very easy to overlook; so if you have a page that's not displaying, you may want to check that it isn't hidden!

Let's just enter *Home Page* as our **Page title** and *Home* as our **Subtitle**, and then click on the save and close button.

Add the Content

Now that we have our first page created, let's add some content to the page. We click on **Page** in the page tree and the page content options are then displayed in the details view on the right.

Under the **NORMAL** heading, we can either click on the small icon with the plus symbol, or the **Create page content** button, as they both do the same thing. The other headings of **LEFT**, **RIGHT**, and **BORDER** add content to different sections of the page, depending on how the page's template is set out. The **NORMAL** heading is for main content, and that is why there is the additional button labeled **Create page content** under this heading.

We then of course want to add a regular text element to our page, although if at this stage your feel comfortable exploring different options and features, you may wish to add text with an image—something that we will cover later in the chapter.

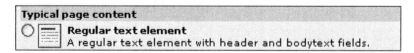

I'm going to add a heading of *Welcome to Durham Electrics*, and a small description of the business for my front page. The built-in **WYSIWYG editor** (What You See Is What You Get) allows us to style our content nicely, without the need for manual HTML coding, in a friendly interface similar to many word processors. You may wish to try out some of the WYSIWYG's features, by adding a table to the content.

View the Page

Right, we now have our first page created, with content! Let's have a look at our work.

If we click on the view-webpage button (the one resembling a magnifying glass) from the page that we are presented with after adding our content, our new web page is opened in a new window.

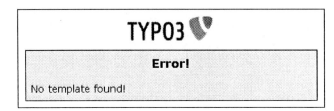

Here, we get an error message. This is because our website does not have a template applied to it. We need a template to add style to our content as we learned in Chapter 3.

Apply the Style

Let us quickly apply a template to the page so we can see it in action, and then take a closer look at the templates available.

While we still have the homepage details in the details view, we can click on the **Template** link from the menu on the left.

This opens the **Template Tools** for the page, and as you can see, we currently have no template assigned to our homepage.

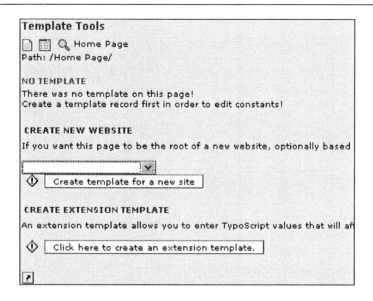

We are going to create a new website, with this home page at the root of it. The template that we assign here will be applied to all further pages created. The template we will use throughout this chapter is the **CrCPH** template, because it is very simple, very easy to modify, and looks quite professional. You may wish to experiment with the templates discussed later, or even download or create your own templates.

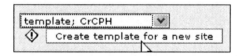

We just need to select the template from the list and click on **Create template for a new site**. We get a prompt that asks **Are you sure you want to do this?**, and we are, so we click on **OK**.

The template is then assigned to the website, and we are taken to a page where we can edit the parameters of the template—something to which we will come back. For now, let's see our website in action at last!

We can of course click on the view web page button (the one with the icon of a magnifying glass) or select **View** from the menu in the page tree.

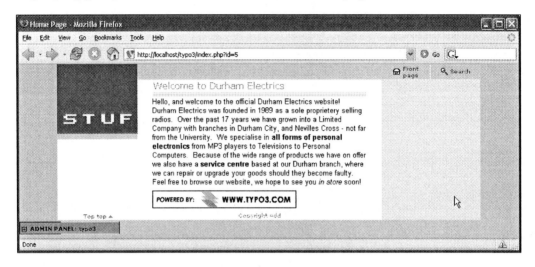

And there we have it! Our web page in action at last!

Templates

There are quite a number of templates pre-installed in TYPO3, which makes it easy to quickly create a new website with a design. Many of the templates have a number of settings to change, to help us easily customize the design of our website.

If you also wish to see which template you prefer, when creating a **New record** select the **Create new page** option. This will create a new root page, as opposed to a sub-page, allowing the page to have its own template. You can then assign the template to the page just as we did with the home page earlier. To add content to the page, you can manage the content in the homepage. Click on the icon next to the content's name (**Welcome to Durham Electrics**) and select **Copy** from the menu. Then click on the new page's name from the page tree and select **Paste Into** to add the content, as we discussed in Chapter 3.

What Templates are Available to Me?

The following templates are available when we install TYPO3:

- Bug
- MM
- Business

- Candidate
- CrCPH
- First
- Glueck
- Green
- Hyper
- Newsletter
- RE
- TU

Most templates have **constants** that can be edited; these are settings that have been created in the templates, but can be changed in the template manager. Constants allow you to change things like: frame sizes, background colors, heading images (complete with an upload function), and other basic design elements of your website. The templates that come with TYPO3 are a little old, and don't conform to the the latest HTML standards; however, they do work and are useful for creating a test site.

Let's take a closer look at the different default templates available!

Template: Bug

This template has three frames: one at the top, one at the left, and one in the middle. A number of the settings of this template are controlled by constants. We can upload a heading image, and set background colors and frame sizes. The menu in the side frame is generated from the sub-pages and is generated as a collection of images. The advantage of having the menu-items generated as images is that we can connect uncommon fonts to the menu, using any font we wish, and the visitor will see the menu exactly as we intended.

Template: MM

This is a very simple, single-column based template. The menu is mapped onto the heading image; so the image that you upload as a heading will have the menu links generated over it. This sort of template isn't the best for displaying a great deal of information, but if you were creating a blog section or something like that, this template is ideal.

Template: Business

This template is a more professional one. A small logo can be added to the side, and the menu is again generated in the left frame. Colors, fonts, and logos can be added through the back end by editing the template's constants.

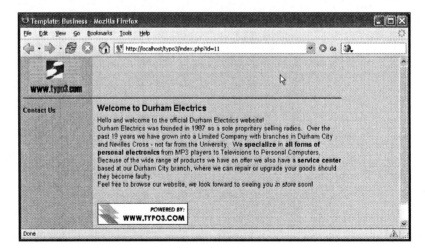

Template: Candidate

Candidate has two content columns, a main one on the left and a smaller one on the right. The menu is text-based and displayed beneath the page heading. Many of the colors and images can be set through constants.

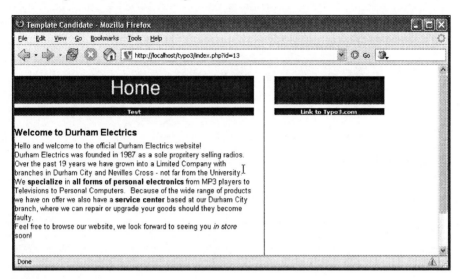

Template: CrCPH

This template works differently from the other pre-installed ones. It is based on an HTML file that can be edited in a text editor to change the style. A few of its aspects can still be changed by editing the template's constants.

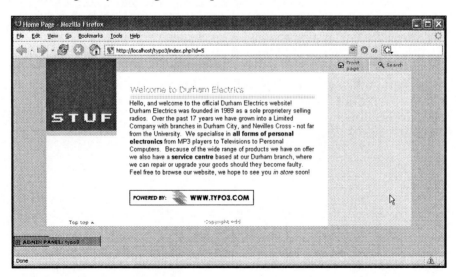

Template: First

This is quite a poor template. The content frames are nested within another frame that centers the whole page. This template seems to load quite slowly, but as with most of the other templates, has a lot of customizable options in the constant editor, including logos, images in different frames, background colors, and frame sizes. The side frame can be set to take content from a separate page. This template uses a graphical menu and a separate general menu in the bottom frame.

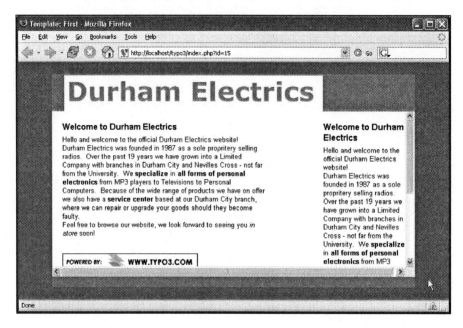

Template: Glueck

Out of the box, this is a very interesting looking template (as you can see from the following screenshot). It has a variety of different backgrounds: a page background, left frame background, main frame background, content frame background within the main frame; and right frame. There are also two places for two different logos, and an optional heading image.

It certainly is very colorful out of the box!

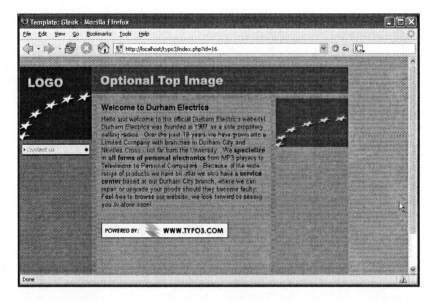

Template: Green

The **Green** template is a very nice simple template, and unsurprisingly it is green! The menu is generated into the header as images. There is a template file containing the basics of the page layout that can be edited too. A professional theme with a green feel! The text is a little difficult to read, however, as it is black on dark green.

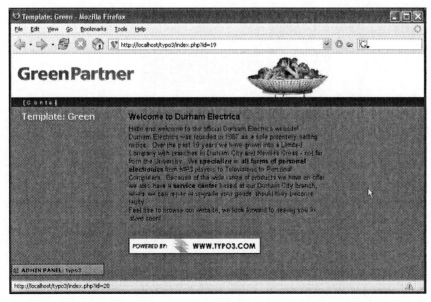

Template: Hyper

Hyper is a different style of template from most of the others, consisting of lots of grid-like images, and horizontal line images. Both the menu and the page title are generated into images and of course a logo can be added to the top left corner. This and other settings are again changed through the template's constants. To be a useable design it would require a lot of modification. The text color is difficult to read as it is black on grey, and the images for background and header clash because of their color difference.

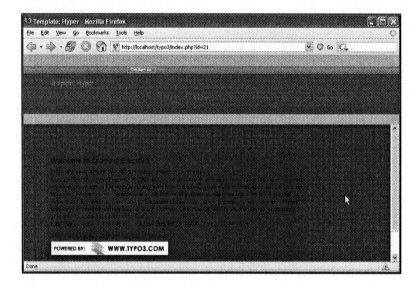

Template: Newsletter

The **Newsletter** template isn't really designed as a template for a whole website, and is more suited to something like—a newsletter surprisingly! It has no menu support, but it does have a simple HTML template that you can edit, a style sheet file that you can edit, a second column for content, a changeable logo, and a changeable copyright notice. The template is designed to be used for newsletters in conjunction with the **Direct Mail** module extension to allow you to email out newsletters directly.

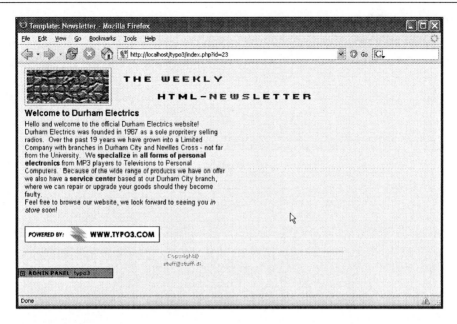

Template: RE

This template has a graphically generated menu beneath the header image, with options for rollover effects when a user places their mouse cursor over the image. There is a left frame taking up the entire height of the window on the left-hand side, with adjustable background and content.

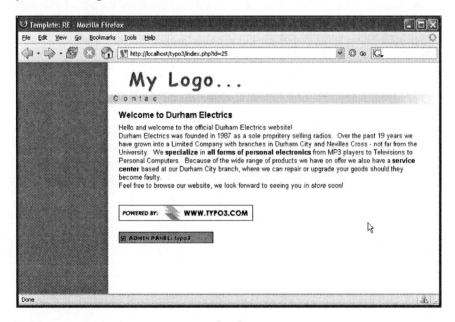

Template: TU

The final template we have is **TU**. This template does not make use of frames, but it does make use of tables to layout its content. There is a graphically generated menu on the left, and we can change the menu's images at the top and bottom (to give a rounded effect), as well as its color. We can add a logo, and change other settings through the template's constants.

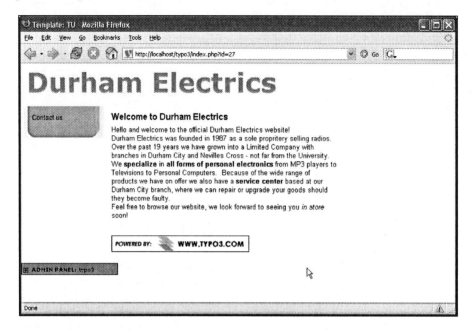

Editing Templates

Now that we have had a look at the templates available to us, let's have a quick look at changing some basic settings in the templates by changing their constants.

When in the **Template** section for a page, there is a menu that allows us to select different sections of the template, including the **Constant Editor**.

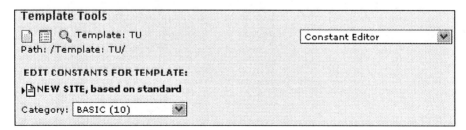

When in the **Constant Editor**, we have two main sections, a **Category** menu, and the actual **Constant Editor** itself. A constant in this sense, *is a setting or variable applied to the template*. For example, page width could have a constant; we could change this to 700px and our page would be that wide. The templates link with the constants to get settings to change their appearance.

The **Category** menu lists the different categories that the constants are divided into. Generally there is a **BASIC** category, a **MENU** category, and a **CONTENT** category, although often there are more.

With constants that relate to something like an image, or menu item, there is often an illustrated screenshot to show how the constant relates to the page. For instance, in the **TU** template we have the following:

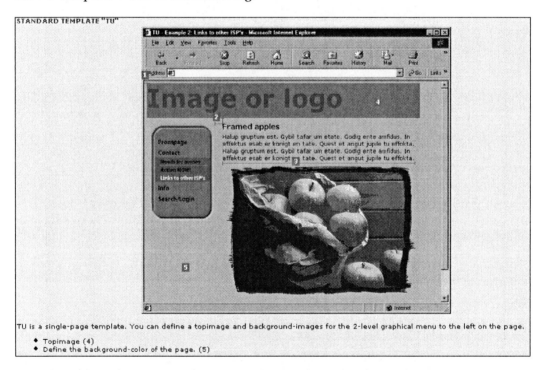

This shows that constant **4** corresponds to the heading image; constant **5** corresponds to the background of the page, and so on.

With the constant editor, we need to select which constants we wish to change before we can change them. If we wish to change the logo and background color, we need to select them to indicate that we are going to change them, and then click on the **Update** button.

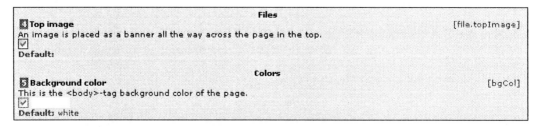

Once we have clicked on the **Update** button, we are presented with text boxes and upload boxes to allow us to change the constants.

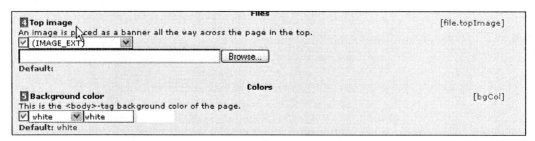

The drop-down box under the **Top image** heading contains all images previously uploaded for this template. If, we change the image later, and wish to change it back it is saved for us.

Once changes have been made to the constants, we just click on the **Update** button again, and the changes are saved.

Returning to the Site

Now that we have explored the templates available, let's return to our website. Throughout the rest of the chapter, I'm going to focus on the template CrCPH, but if you feel up to it, you may wish to try applying a different template and working with that.

The Contact Page

We have our home page completed, so let's create the *contact* page. This page needs to do two functions; firstly it needs to convey the different contact methods available, and it also needs to contain an online form that will allow visitors to email us directly from the site.

We create the new sub-page by clicking on the **Home Page** icon, and selecting **New**.

Then we want to create a new **Page (Inside)** to create the sub-page. Once we have created the page, and given it a name and saved it, we want to add the two content elements.

We can add the main content in the same way that we added the content to the homepage earlier on, using a **Regular text element**.

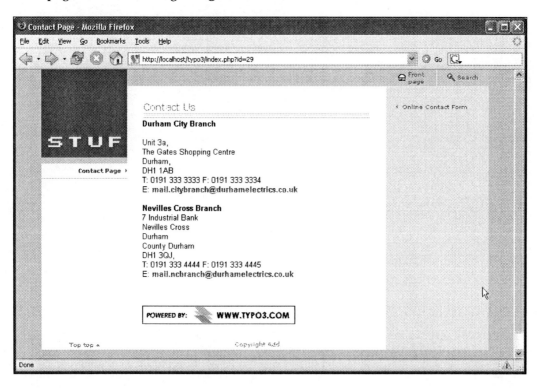

After adding the static content details, I've decided to add my contact form to a separate page, which will be a sub-page of the contact page. You may, however, prefer to add it as a separate content element on the same page, depending on your preferences or the template you are using. Since this is a sub-page of the contact page, we need to click on the contact page button and select new page, and then click on **Page (Inside)**.

Instead of adding a **Regular text element** to the page, we now want to add a **Mail form** to the page.

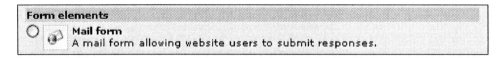

The **Mail form** allows us to create a form that will then send us an email with the information users have submitted to the website, and then redirect them to a new page. We could create a thank you page to send them to.

The configuration for the form needs to be changed slightly as by default it only asks for the user's name, email address, and postal address. It's easy enough to change the address details to make it an area for the user to type a message.

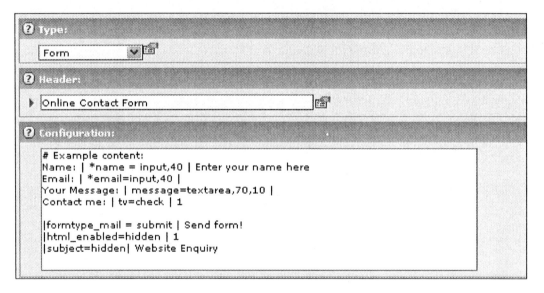

I've left my form at that, but you may wish to add more options. There is a forms wizard that can help you create and edit the form. It can be accessed by clicking on the **Forms wizard** button next to the configuration box.

 You will need to save the page first, and then return to edit the content element to see the **Form wizard** button!

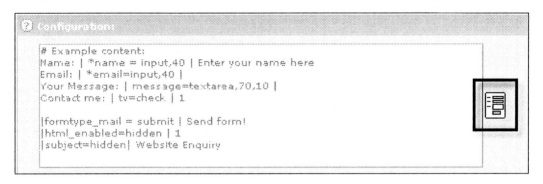

The wizard has options to allow us to add new field rows, delete existing fields, and modify existing fields, as well as change the email address that the contact form submission is sent to.

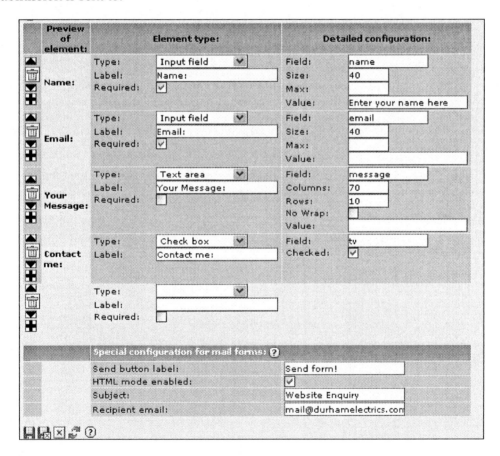

Once our form is saved, we can view the page and see our contact form.

If you have installed TYPO3 locally on your machine, it is most likely that this form will not work if you test it. This is because you may not have a local mail server installed. If you have it installed on a proper web server or some local Linux workstations, then the email should send.

The Search Page

Good navigation and search facilities are key to a useful website. Having content is great—so long as people can actually find it. We will create a new sub-page from the homepage and call it *Search Page*. The page content of course will be the **Search form**.

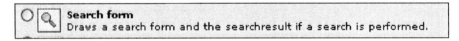

The only field that we need to complete is the heading, and then we can see the search result in action.

The search page provides two search options. We can search page headings and keywords (keywords are defined with advanced pages) or search actual page content.

I'm going to type in a search for *Nevilles* which is a part of the address in one of the content elements on the contact page.

Performing the search then displays a list of pages where the word was found as well as an excerpt from the page content element.

Products and Services Pages

Following the website structure defined earlier, we should create a page for products, and a page for services, each of these having sub-pages for the specific services or product groups.

We've been through this process a few times now, so I'll let you create those on your own. Once completed, the website structure for these sections should look something like this:

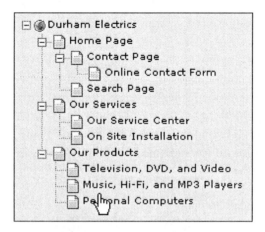

Customer-Only Area

Creating a customer-only area is a little trickier than the other sections that we have added.

We need to create:

- A login form
- A protected page
- A user group
- Some customer user accounts

Creating the User Groups and Customer Accounts

Before we can actually create the user group and customer user names, we need a place to store them. We need to create a new page within our website, but instead of it being a standard page, we change it to a **SysFolder** type.

A **SysFolder** is a TYPO3 folder that contains system information, in this case, user groups. Other folders contain files and content.

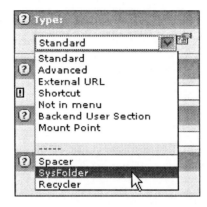

We can then name this folder something like **Users and Groups**. Because we are working with users and groups, we want the folder to contain the **Website Users** plugin. So we select **Website Users** from the **Contains plugin** menu.

Once this has been created we need to make a note of its ID number for later. If we hover the mouse cursor over the folder in the page tree, we will see the ID number. The folder I have created has an ID of 43, as shown below

Now that we have our system folder, we can create our users and groups. To do so, we need to click on the folder icon and select **New** from the menu that pops up.

The **New record** screen for the system folder is slightly different from the other **New record** screens that we have seen. This is because we have had to select the **Website users** plugin and it allows us to create a new **Website user** and **Website usergroup**.

We need to create a new group, by clicking on the **Website usergroup** link and then entering the name of the group. I have chosen customers as the name of my usergroup. Once we have our customer group, we can create a new **Website user** who will have permission to log in to the customer-only section of the website.

We enter a username and a password, and then select the group from the group list:

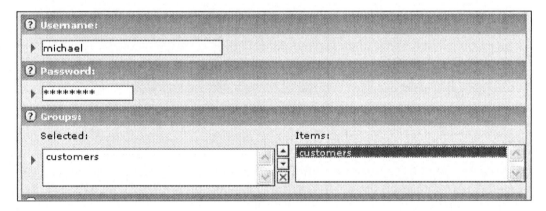

Creating a Protected Page

Now that we have our customer group and a user to log in, we can create our protected page. When creating a new page for the customer-only section, we can specify if we wish the page to be hidden from the menu, as it is possible to get the page to display once a user has logged in.

The **General options** provide access restrictions, allowing us to restrict the page to members of the customers group.

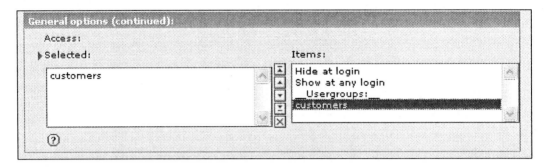

The other two options here, **Hide at login** and **Show at any login**, would allow us to hide the content when the user logs in—for instance we could hide a login box when the user logs in. We could also set something to show at login, which would display regardless of the user's group, when they logged in.

Creating the Login Page

We can either have a separate page for logging in, or we can just add the login form as a content element to an existing page. The **Login form** element is grouped with the other **Form elements** in the **New content element** page.

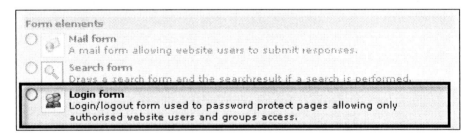

The **Login form** element asks us for a heading, and also for a **Send to page:** option. If we leave the **Send to page:** option empty, the login form will return us to whichever page the login element is on, otherwise it will take us to the page that we specify. To specify the page we can click the folder icon to see the pages available.

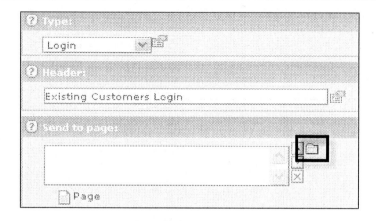

This opens up a pop-up window with the pages listed within, and so, we can select the page from here:

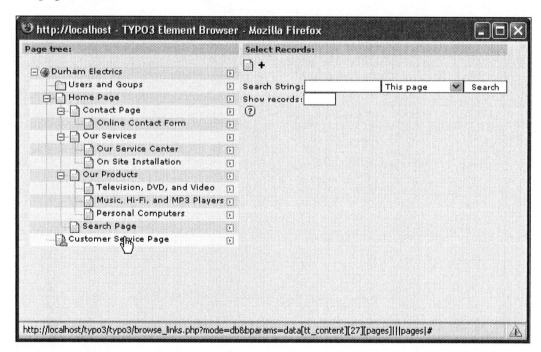

Clicking on the page we wish to be transferred to in here will automatically populate the field in the page we were in, creating the login element. We can then save the page.

One final thing that we need to do here, is to tell the login page where the sysfolder containing our users is stored. With the login page still open in the back end, we need to click on the **Template** section from within the **Web** module, select the **Constant Editor** from the drop-down box at the top right, and select the **CONTENT** category from the drop-down box in the middle of the page. In here, we need to edit the **PID of user archive** option, by ticking the checkbox next to it and then clicking on the **Update** button at the bottom of the page.

Content: 'Login'

PID of user archive [styles.content.loginform.pid]
Enter the page-uid number (PID) of the sysFolder where you keep your fe_users that are supposed to login on this site. This setting is necessary, if login is going to work!
☑43 Range: 0 -
Default:

The page then reloads, with a text box next to the checkbox. We enter the ID of the system folder that we made a note of earlier, before clicking on **Update** again. Once the page has reloaded, we need to scroll to the bottom, and click on the link to **clear all cache**. This will apply the new setting to the page.

Customer-Only Area in Action

I created my login form as part of the homepage, so on the homepage I have the form.

Existing Customers Login

Username:

Password:

Login

And when I log in, I am taken to the customer page:

Welcome!

Welcome to our existing customers!

Customizing our Template

Now that our website has been created, let's return again to the templates, to tweak the design of our website.

The main advantage of the template that we are using is that the bulk of the layout can be changed from the template file. In the template manager, we can edit some basic settings by changing the constants. The most notable constant for this particular template is **Template file** because it allows us to refresh the template with the template file, should we make any changes to it, or to refresh from a copy of the file stored elsewhere.

The value of this particular constant is by default: `typo3/sysext/cms/tslib/media/uploads/crcph/main.htm`. This is the location in the TYPO3 installation of the template file. Let's make a copy of this file to edit with a text editor.

```
16
17  </head>
18
19  <body bgcolor="#D6D3CE" text="#333333" leftmargin="0" topmargin="0" marginwidth="0" marginheight="0" lin
20  <!-- ###DOCUMENT_BODY### start-->
21  <table width="778" border="0" bgcolor="#FFFFFF" cellspacing="0" cellpadding="0" align="center">
22    <tr>
23      <td align="left" valign="top" rowspan="3">
24        <table width="1" border="0" cellpadding="0" cellspacing="0">
25          <tr valign="middle">
26            <td height="22" colspan="2" align="center"> <a name="top"></a><a href="index.php?id=123"><img
27          </tr>
28          <tr valign="middle" bgcolor="#CEDBDE">
29            <td height="10" colspan="2" align="center"><img src="clear.gif" width="10" height="10" alt=""
30          </tr>
31
32      <!-- ###SUB_MENU### start
33          This surrounds all the menuitems, substituted with the dynamic menu
34      -->
35
36      <!-- ###SUB_MENU_ITEM### begin
37          This is a single menu item
38      -->
```

The text that is wrapped in '###' tags indicates values or sections that are replaced dynamically by TYPO3. These are called **markers** when they appear on their own, and **subparts** when they appear in pairs. We can customize this file as much as we wish, but should be careful not to delete any important TYPO3 comments as these are required for TYPO3 to process the Template.

I'm going to edit the location of the logo (as this template does not have the ability for us to upload a new logo from the constant editor), and the copyright notice.

There are one or two links that we need to edit, as they are hard coded into the template file and are not correct. The links for the homepage point to a page with an ID of 123 and the links for the search page point to a page with an ID of 987, neither of which exist for me, nor if they did exist would they be the home and search pages

To find out the ID numbers of the homepage and search page, we can place our mouse cursor over the page icon for those pages in the TYPO3 back end, and the ID number is displayed.

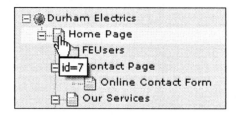

The colors and other basic settings can be left as they are, as we can change them through the constant editor.

Once changes have been made to the template, we need to reload the template file from the constant editor. Tick the box for **Template file** and click on **Update**.

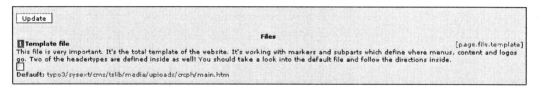

We can then either select the file from the list, or upload a copy of the file so that we can revert between styles later.

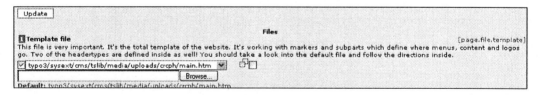

With the logo, copyright notice, and link changes I have made, my website now looks like this:

Versioning

The versioning tools can be grouped into two categories, per-user tools (which affect the user and how they manage content), and the content itself (you can create and manage versions of the content). Here we will look at the tools for the content themselves, and we will look at the user-centric content-versioning tools in Chapter 6.

We can use versioning for a number of different things:

- Creating new versions of content ready to be swapped into place
- Managing content changes
- Restricting who can edit live changes, but allowing them to edit a copy of a live version—something we will see in Chapter 6

If we select versioning from a page's menu, we are taken to the page's versioning management section.

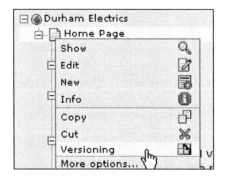

The versioning page itself lists the versions of the page and allows us to create new versions of either the page and content, all sub-pages, or just the record of the page.

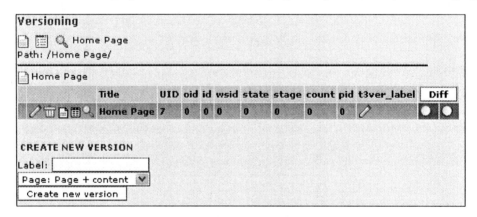

If we create a new version of the page, we can modify that page, and then bring it into effect whenever we wish, by clicking on the **SWAP with current** button.

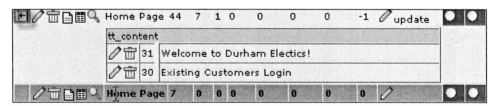

If we create a new revision of the branch, which includes all of the page's sub-pages, we can modify each page individually, and then roll out all of the changes in an instant with the **SWAP with current** button.

Each page, sub-page, and content element is listed with the branch, so we can easily select which section of a version we are changing.

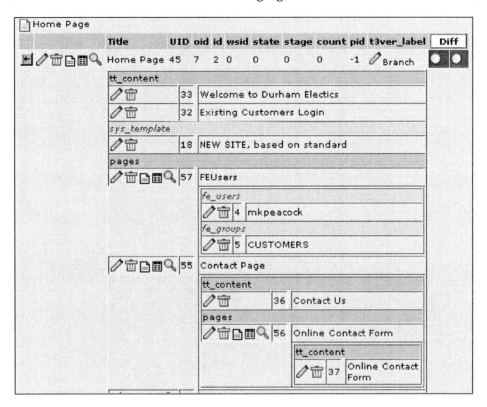

Summary

In this chapter we have applied our knowledge of the TYPO3 administration features, which we looked at in Chapter 3, to the website scenario we discussed in Chapter 1.

We created the website, looking at how the pages fit together, how to get the pages to display, how to customize the design and how to manage different versions of the content.

Now that we have toured the administration panel and set up our website, it is time to look at the features available for us in the front end to allow us to easily change and manage the website and its content.

5

Front-End Features

We now have our website up and running and we know how to manage the content from the website's back end. It is now time for us to look into the various front-end features available to us. In this chapter, we will learn:

- What front-end tools are available
- What front-end tools do
- How to edit and publish from the front end

In order to access the front-end tools, we must first log in to the back end of TYPO3. Once logged in, we can then return to the front end of the website. From the front end we will see that there is an **ADMIN PANEL** section at the bottom of each page; this is a feature, which is enabled by default with our template. Here is our **ADMIN PANEL**:

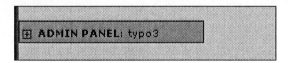

Front-End Admin Panel Overview

The front-end admin panel is divided into a number of sections:

- Preview
- Cache
- Publish
- Editing
- TypoScript
- Info

We can show and hide different sections of our **ADMIN PANEL** using the + and – buttons displayed next to the relevant titles, as shown in the following screenshot:

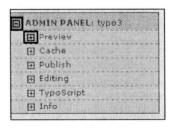

Unfortunately, a limitation of the front-end admin panel is that when you try to expand or collapse a section of the admin panel (using the + and – icons) the page has to be reloaded for the new sections to show or hide themselves. I would recommend that you leave frequently used sections expanded, and just hide the entire panel when you don't want to use it, as showing the panel again will expand all of the sections you had expanded previously. These preferences are stored in the TYPO3 database, and only need to be set once, not each time you log in using another computer.

Once we have opened a particular section of our **ADMIN PANEL**, an **Update** button will appear at the top of the panel to allow us to save the setting changes we have made.

Preview

The preview features allow us to change the conditions, which changes the content we can see. The features are as shown in the following screenshot:

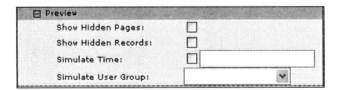

The conditions that we can change are as follows:

- Ability to see hidden pages.
- Ability to see hidden content elements, i.e. records.
- Time—as some pages are time-sensitive, we can simulate an alternative time to see what content would be available to us.
- Usergroup—as content can be restricted to specific usergroups, we can simulate a different user group and see content that would be available if we were logged in as a member of that particular group.

When we change these conditions, the pages that were not accessible to us before (i.e., hidden or time-sensitive) are displayed, with a **PREVIEW** box to inform us that we are previewing the page by changing the conditions. This **PREVIEW** box is also displayed when we view a hidden page directly from the back end by clicking **View Page** on a hidden page. Here is the **PREVIEW** box:

Hidden Pages

Let's take a look at the hidden page setting to view content that is not live. First, let's create a page and set the visibility to hidden.

In Chapters 3 and 4 we learned how to create pages and toggle the visibility of the pages; so let's apply that knowledge here, by creating a hidden content element on the page and by creating a separate page that is also hidden.

Now that we have some hidden content, its time to change the conditions for viewing the page. We will set the **Show Hidden Pages** option, as shown in the screenshot:

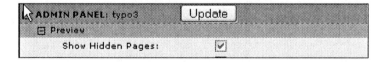

Once we have changed the setting and clicked the **Update** button, the page will reload to reflect the changes. Here is the screenshot:

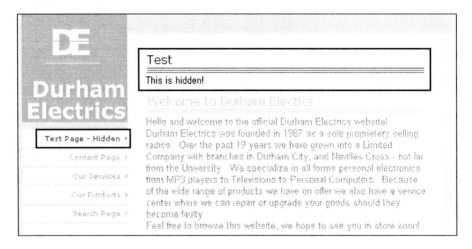

Reminder: Page and Page Content Visibility

When we create a new page, the page is automatically set to be invisible, as the check box in the new page is already checked. This is how it appears on our screen:

We can toggle the visibility of a page or page content by clicking on the icon for the page or content element and selecting **Hide/Unhide**. It is shown in the following screenshot:

Hidden Records

The hidden records option is similar to the hidden pages option, except that it can also show content such as alternative language content, or content that is hidden by template settings (TypoScript).

Time-Sensitive Content

We can create content that is time sensitive, which is useful if we want to prepare information on a sale or special offer that is only valid for a set period of time.

To see how this feature works, we need to first create some time-sensitive content. If we create a new content element in the back end, there are some **General options**, which contain the time-sensitivity options. For example, I'll set the time frame for a weekend to inform the visitor that there is a special offer over the weekend. Here is the screenshot:

Now that we have some time-sensitive content on the front page, we can simulate the time by entering it into the **Simulate Time** field and clicking the **Update** button, to see the content. We will get a similar screen to this:

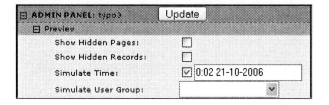

With the time now simulated to be within the special offer time frame, we can see the content which was hidden:

Usergroup-Sensitive Content

We already have usergroup-sensitive content on our website, as we have a login box on the front page, and a special customer service page. If we simulate the **CUSTOMERS** group, we should be able to see this content automatically without the need to log in to the website.

We need to select the **Simulate User Group** option from the list:

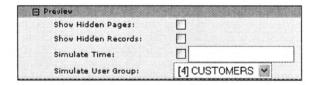

Then update the settings with the **Update** button shown in the following screenshot:

After clicking the **Update** button, the page will reload. The changes are then reflected instantly, as we are logged in (although no username is displayed) and we have the **Customer Service Page** on the menu, which we can access and view now. Here is the screenshot:

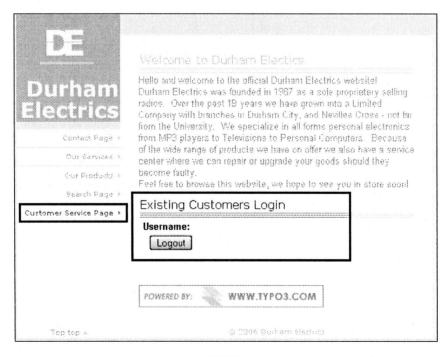

Cache

The cache settings allow us to change and refresh TYPO3's cache. This cache has various settings and data stored temporarily on the server. After major system changes, the cache needs to be cleared so that new data or settings can be applied correctly. Having a cache decreases the time taken for pages to load, as TYPO3 processes information such as settings or image functions (especially true with image-generated menus in some templates). It then stores the end result in the cache, saving the need for the system to process these tasks on each page load. We will get a similar screen to this:

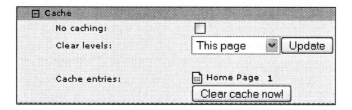

We can turn off the cache here, clear the cache for various page levels, and clear the cache for the current page. It also details the number of cache entries for the current page, and as you can see, with the settings and template we have used in the example website, no cache records are created.

Pages are structured in levels; we have our home page, and the other pages are sub-pages, which makes them one level below (as you can see from the tree structure in the back end). We can select an option just to clear this page, or clear this page and all other pages within its level or one level below i.e., all of the other pages we have created, as these are sub-pages.

Publishing

The publishing section allows us to publish our TYPO3 pages into static HTML pages (we will set the output directory later). This can have several uses:

- We can create pages to be archived or mirrored elsewhere.
- We can speed up page generation, as no business logic needs to be processed on page load.

Unfortunately, the links created are as they were on the live site, and do not point to the published copies. If we were to publish our website to an archive, or wanted the published pages to be used on our live site (as we don't have any dynamic content), we would need to change the links and menu manually to reflect the published pages. Here is the screenshot:

The publishing options allow us to publish a specific page, or the page and several sub-levels below. For example if we select **+ 1 sublevel** from the **Publish levels** drop-down box, this would convert the home page and all of the subpages we have created (such as the contact page, and the products and services pages) into static HTML files, which are then sent into a designated publish directory.

Setting the Publish Directory

Before we actually publish any of the pages, we need to tell TYPO3 where we wish for it to create the static pages. If we go to the back end, and select **Configuration** from the **Tools** menu, as shown, we can see and change the publish_dir setting:

Within the configuration tool, we can see the publish_dir setting under the **FE** section; this setting currently has no value assigned to it. Here is the screenshot for the settings:

```
$TYPO3_CONF_VARS
  [GFX]
  [SYS]
  [EXT]
  [BE]
  [FE]
      [png_to_gif]=0
      [tidy]=0
      [tidy_option]=cached
      [tidy_path]=tidy -i --quiet true --tidy-mark true --wrap 0 -raw
      [logfile_dir]=
      [publish_dir]=
```

Unfortunately, the configuration data cannot actually be set from the TYPO3 back end, but it will tell us how we should amend the configuration file. If we click on the `publish_dir` setting, a variable dialog appears with the correct structure for the setting, which we can change; but then we must copy the value in its entirety and paste it into the configuration file itself. This is shown in the following screenshot:

```
Variable:
$TYPO3_CONF_VARS['FE']['publish_dir'] = '/';
(Now, copy/paste this value into the configuration file where you can set it. This is all you can do from here...)
```

 Note: I have selected '/' as `publish_dir` because linked resources such as images will not be copied; only the pages are copied into a static format. This means if we published to a new folder, none of the images would appear and we would have to copy them manually to our publish directory.

We then copy the code into the `localconf.php` configuration file, which, provided we ran a default install of the TYPO3 Winstaller, should be located at: `c:\Program Files\Typo3 4.0.2\Apache\typo3_src\typo3conf\`.

We can just open this file with a text editor, such as Notepad, and then paste the following code in the relevant line of code:

```
$TYPO3_CONF_VARS['FE']['publish_dir'] = '/';
```

Here is the screenshot showing where to place the code:

```
29  $TYPO3_CONF_VARS['BE']['staticFileEditPath'] = 'fileadmin/static/'; //   Modified or inserted by TYPO3
30
31  $TYPO3_CONF_VARS['FE']['publish_dir'] = '/';     //   Modified or inserted by TYPO3 Install Tool.
32
33  // Updated by TYPO3 Install Tool 11-03-2006 12:11:58
```

Once we have pasted the code, we can save and close the file, and actually use the publishing feature of TYPO3.

If we publish our **Home Page** by clicking the **Publish now** button from the **admin panel**, the page will reload, and we will get a message telling us that the page has been published, as shown in the following screenshot:

Publishing in: /|
Writing: /7.0.html|

We can then visit the static HTML page using the following address: http://localhost/typo3/7.0.html, where 7.0.html is the file into which TYPO3 has written.

Editing

One of the most useful and important features of the TYPO3 front end is that of front-end editing. We can edit and create content for our website directly from within the website itself, without the need to navigate to the TYPO3 back end. The content-editing features available here are the same as in the back end. You may find it more useful to use front-end editing if you spot a mistake you wish to amend, or to help you visualize where you wish to make changes. The back end is generally more useful when performing other tasks at the same time, such as managing users.

This section of the admin panel has a number of options and settings available to let us customize our front-end editing, as shown in the following screenshot:

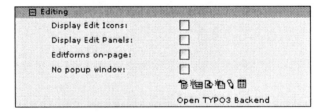

Front-End Editing—Settings

Let's see what the different settings for front-end editing do:

- **Display Edit Icons**: This setting adds small pencil icons to the various content elements on the page, which when clicked will allow you to edit the element.

- **Display Edit Panels**: This adds other icons, like a tool bar, to the page, which gives the ability to move content around on a page and edit the page itself.

- **Editforms on-page**: As opposed to opening in a pop-up window or opening an edit form in a new page, this will reload the page with the edit form embedded into the current page.
- **No popup window**: If the edit form is not set to be on-page, then a pop-up window opens with the edit form in. This option will prevent the pop-up window opening, instead reloading the page and replacing it with an edit form.

Front-End Editing—Links

In addition to the setting for editing in the admin panel, there are also some links to various pages, as shown in the following screenshot:

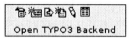

Going from left to right, these links allow us to do the following:

- View the record change history of the page.
- Create a new content element.
- Move the page.
- Create a new page.
- Edit page properties.
- View the **Web | List** module.

Beneath the icons, there is a link to take us to the back end.

Front-End Editing

Now that we know what front-end editing features and tools are available, we can see some of them in action.

In order to see all of the appropriate options for the content and to prevent unnecessary pop-up windows, I've selected all the four options in the editing panel. With these settings, there are several editing options that have now appeared on the page. There are some page editing options at the top, and then beneath the first content element there is the edit button, which will allow us to edit the content itself. Beneath that there are options for that particular element, such as delete, move, and edit. Here is the screenshot showing all the options:

In order to edit inline text (open the editing pane within the page itself), we need to use the edit icon that is grouped with the other properties icons, as the separate edit icon will either open a new page or open a pop-up window if that option is not selected.

Here is a screenshot displaying the result:

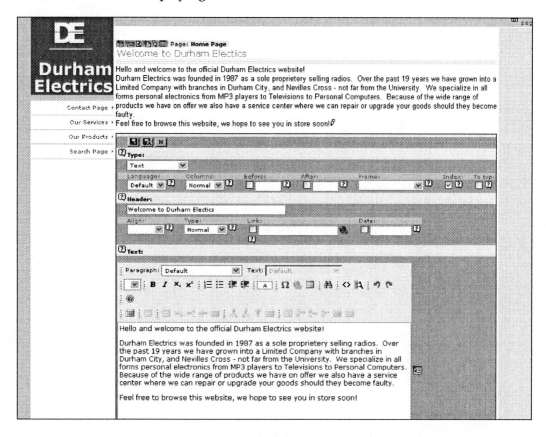

We can see the content that we are editing, and then we can edit the content in the edit section beneath it, and save it. This makes it really easy, especially for users who don't edit or use the system frequently—they might browse the site, and see a spelling mistake or realize that something is missing, and just click the edit button to make the change.

TypoScript

The TYPO3 template engine utilizes advanced features using something called TypoScript, TYPO3's built-in configuration mechanism. This is used to generate image menus and dynamic content within the templates.

 These settings are primarily useful when working with complex templates. With the template we have been using, these features have little benefit to us.

The following screenshot displays all the options we have:

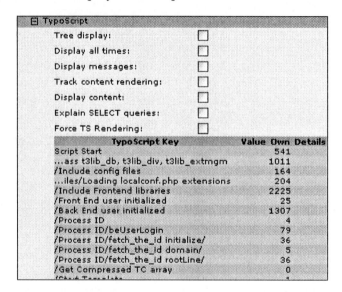

The various settings change the information that we can see in the following screenshot. **Tree display** will convert the TypoScript table below it (the table with **TypoScript Key**, **Value,** etc.) to represent a tree structure showing how the various TypoScript Keys relate to one another, as shown in the screenshot on the next page:

TypoScript Key	Value	Own Details
Script Start		16
......ass t3lib_db, t3lib_div, t3lib_extmgm		269
/Include config files		68
......php extensions		78
/Include Frontend libraries		245
/Front End user initialized		16
/Back End user initialized		399
/Process ID		4
/Process ID/beUserLogin		9
/Process ID/fetch_the_id initialize/		12
/Process ID/fetch_the_id domain/		3
/Process ID/fetch_the_id rootLine/		8
/Get Compressed TC array		0
/Start Template		0
/Get Page from cache		9
/Get Page from cache/Cache Row		0
......Page from cache/Cache Row/Cache Query		3
/Parse template		88
/Setting the config-array		1
/Page generation		835
/Page generation/Cache Query		3
php, initialize		1
php, render		0
page	PAGE	393
/substituteMarkerArray/		3
/substituteMarkerArray/		0
/substituteMarkerArray/		4
/substituteMarkerArray/		3
/substituteMarkerArray/		1
/substituteMarkerArray/		1
/substituteMarkerArray/		0
/substituteMarkerArray/		5
/substituteMarkerArray/		0
/Page generation/Tidy, cached		0
/Print Content		1
/Stat		0

In this tree, we can see how the page is generated. It outlines various files or functions that TYPO3 includes, shows processes and logic that it must perform, and gets the data and the templates and then combines the two by rendering the page.

If we have the time display setting, then it will add a time field to the table; so we can see how long it takes for various things to be processed. This can be useful if we find our page is loading slowly, and if it turns out that we have a complex image generation script that is taking up most of the time, we can isolate the problem.

The messages and content rendering options require the tree display to be enabled, as they extend the information displayed to us. The results of these options produce a huge table, too big to be included here, as the table is too detailed, try the options out for yourself to see the information it displays.

Info

Finally, we have the **Info** section. It displays some general information about the page we are viewing. We have the page ID number; we can see that the page is not being stored in the TYPO3 cache, and if we were logged in as a front-end user, we would see the username and user ID. Finally, we can see how long it has taken TYPO3 to generate and display the page. Here is the screenshot displaying the **Info** section:

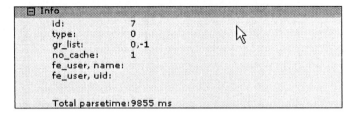

Summary

We have looked at the features that are offered by the TYPO3 front end, in particular the front-end editing features available. We have learned how these features work, what they do, and how we can edit and create content for our website directly from the website itself, without navigating through the back end.

6
User Management

We now have our website up and running, and we know how to manage the content from both the front end and the back end of TYPO3. It is now time for us to look at user management so that others can work with and manage our website. In this chapter, we will learn:

- How to create and manage user accounts
- How to create usergroups
- Setting user permissions
- User preferences

User Preferences

Before we go looking into creating and managing other users, let's have a detailed look at our user preferences, which we briefly looked at in Chapter 3.

In the TYPO3 back end, our preferences are stored under the **Setup** section of the **User** module, as shown in the following screenshot:

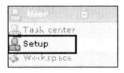

From here we can:

- Simulate another user — which effectively logs us in to the back end as them, without disclosing their password and allowing us to quickly swap back
- Change our language
- Edit our preferences when TYPO3 starts up

- Change some advanced file copy and delete preferences
- Change our content editing preferences
- Change our personal details
- Reset preferences to their default values

Simulation and Language

Provided we are logged in as an administrator, the first two options available to us are to **Simulate backend user** and to change our **LANGUAGE**. The options are shown in the following screenshot:

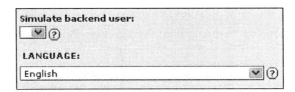

The back-end user simulation allows us to access the back end as if we were logged in as another user. There are a number of reasons for this. User passwords are stored as MD5 hashes, which is an irreversible one way hashing, and not stored in a readable form. So, we cannot see what the password is, which is good for security. If we could see the password, it would be very time consuming to log out, log in as the other user, then log out and log back in as ourselves.

In order to change the settings of another user, we must actually simulate that user and then make the changes, making it more difficult to accidentally change a user's preferences or details. This is also useful if the users are complaining that they are unable to access or do something in the back end that they should be allowed to do. We can then log in as them to investigate the problem properly.

We can also change the back-end language, so all text in the back end is displayed in the user's preferred language.

Start Up

We can also change how the back end is structured when we log in to it. The structure is shown in the following screenshot:

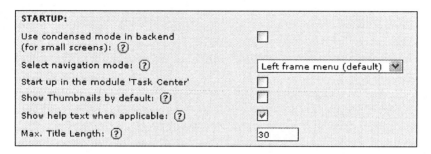

Condensed mode in the back end will load the back end with all of the modules having their menu items folded up, so we have to manually open them and then select the sub-module within that we want to use. It is useful for users with small screens, or if we want to try to reduce the start-up time of the back end (slightly); otherwise it is an inconvenience.

The TYPO3 back end has three separate navigation modes; which you use is down to personal preference.

Firstly, there is the default and the most commonly used left-frame menu option, as shown in the previous screenshot. When we save this configuration and follow the instruction given on the same page, we get a similar screen to this:

Then, there is selector box in the top frame, which removes the side menu and adds a drop-down selection box next to the **TYPO3** logo at the top. Here is the screenshot:

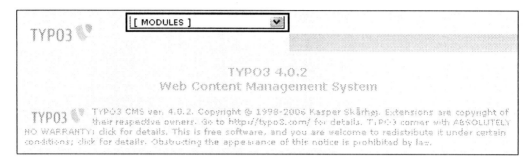

The menu expands to give us all these options:

Then, there are icons in top frame layout, which removes the left menu and places a line of icons to the top of the page. To show which sub-module we are viewing, the respective icon has a border around it, and each icon has a tool tip to explain what it links to. The icons are shown in the screenshot below:

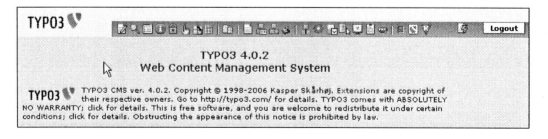

We also have the option to start TYPO3 in the **Task center**. This will automatically take us to the **Task center** when we log in to TYPO3. This option is useful to check for tasks assigned to us or notes we may have left. We could force each user to be taken to the **Task center,** when they enter the back end, with some settings in the TSconfig section of the user or group. This will be covered later in the chapter.

If we have the **Show Thumbnails by default** option enabled, then when we view our website in the **List** mode (see the **Web | List** sub-module), we can see the attached images as inline thumbnails while browsing the list.

We have the **Show help text when applicable** option, which will automatically put help information on some pages to assist with some of the features in the back end.

The final option in the startup section of the user preferences is the **Max. Title Length** that limits the length of titles displayed in page trees. For instance, if we have long page titles, they can cramp and obscure our file structure tree by occupying several lines. By default this value is set to 30, I have set mine to 10, in order to explain the features more thoroughly. Setting this value, we will get a similar screen to this:

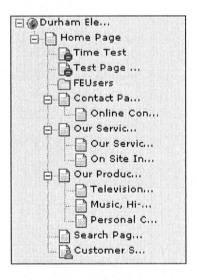

Here page titles longer than a total of 10 characters are limited only to the first ten characters followed by "...", making a much cleaner view and user interface.

Advanced Functions

There are two **Advanced Functions**. These are preferences that we can change, both of which are similar:

- **Recursive Copy**
- **Recursive Delete**

The preferences are shown in the screenshot:

The **Recursive Copy** setting allows us to set the number of page levels we want to copy when we copy a page. If we set this to 1, then this would copy one sublevel too. Currently, all of our pages in our website are in a sublevel to the home page. With this set to 1, if we were to copy the home page and paste a copy of it alongside it, it would also copy all pages in the first sublevel, such as the contact and services pages (individual products are set at a level further below and would not be copied).

We can also recursively delete files. With this setting enabled, when we delete a page, it will also delete all sub-pages. It is useful if we need to remove a whole section of our website frequently.

Edit

There are also a number of preferences that we may change here. These affect editing data in TYPO3. The preferences are shown in the screenshot:

If we enable the option to have a **Wide document background**, the form width will be increased by about 50%. This would give us more room to work while editing content and data.

The option **Enable Rich Text Editor (if available)** is set by default. This gives us a *What You See Is What You Get* (WYSIWIG) style editor, where we see the content's format being changed as we make the changes. It means that when we click the bold button and then type some more text into the text area, the text will appear as bold in the text area.

The file upload option will enable a file upload box on records and allows files to be attached. If we disable this option, then the file upload box will still be displayed on the relevant pages, but it will not work.

TYPO3 has a large number of built-in help features, which we have looked at in earlier chapters; one of the most useful help features is the inline help. This inline help has two options: we can either see a help icon (a question mark in a circle), or we can see a full text message instead. Personally, I prefer the use of the help icon only, as the presence of icon alerts me to the fact that there is help available on a particular feature, and clicking the icon will provide me with the help, reducing clutter on the screen.

In the web module, we get a special menu when we click on any of the elements in the website's tree view, this is known as a Context Menu. This can be disabled if we want, using the **Disable Popup Context Menus** setting.

Personal Data

Finally, we have our personal data, which has a number of uses. The **PERSONAL DATA** setting is shown in the screenshot:

The **Your name** option is useful when we have lot of users, and need to know what they are called. Users can edit their names themselves, so it is useful in the case of a spelling mistake or a name change. We can enter our email address, which in turn enables us to activate the security setting to send an email when someone logs into TYPO3 using our account. This notification is a great security feature, especially if we rarely log in to TYPO3 using the main administrator account, as we will get an email to tell us someone is using the system.

This is also useful when we use the task center's messaging module, so that messages can be emailed directly to the user they are being sent to. The disadvantage of this is that if we frequently log in to TYPO3 with this account, then we will get lots of emails regarding this.

Once we are happy with the changes, we can click on the **Save Configuration** option:

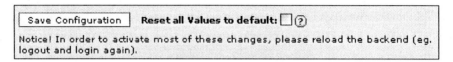

We have a number of changes to be made, such as the back-end layout options, that will take effect only if we log out and then log back in again. If we wish to reset all of the values back to their original values, we can check the **Reset all Values to default** box to do this for us.

Creating Usergroups

Back-end users, the users that can access the TYPO3 back end, are grouped together into back-end groups. These users can access the front-end editing features, but are not front-end users. A group allows us to have specific settings and permissions that its users will automatically use, and also allows us to organize our users easily. These back-end usergroups are for users who have access to the TYPO3 back end. As we are going through this section, you may wish to create a group of your own, such as Editors or Product Managers, and think what permissions and settings would be appropriate for them.

To create a new usergroup, we need to go to the **New record** screen, which can be done by clicking **New** from the menu generated when we click the globe icon at the top of the list view, as shown:

From the **New record** screen, we can create a new back-end usergroup by selecting the option shown in the following screenshot:

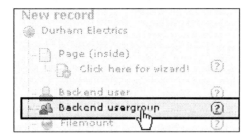

This will take us to the form to create a new back-end usergroup, which provides us with a number of options:

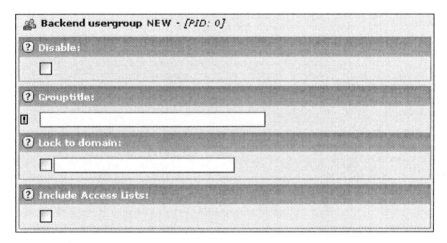

The first four options are **Disable, Grouptitle, Lock to domain**, and **Include Access Lists**.

The **Disable** option will prevent all users who are part of this usergroup inheriting any of the permissions and settings that are defined in the group's settings.

The **Grouptitle** is mandatory, as denoted by the yellow square containing an exclamation mark next to the field. It is just a text description so we know what the purpose of the group is. Possible names for groups could be Editors, News Writers, etc.

One of the features of TYPO3 is that we can have a number of separate websites and/or separate domains running from the same installation of TYPO3. Because of this, we may wish to restrict some users to particular websites or domains. The **Lock to domain** option allows us to specify the domain to which a usergroup is restricted to. This domain will be the only one that users of this group can log in through, and will be the only website they can access and edit. If users are not locked to a domain, then they have access to all the domains.

If we select the **Include Access Lists** option, the page will reload containing a number of permission options that are available to the usergroup.

Include Access Lists

The **Include Access Lists** option gives us eight new areas to configure when creating the group. This option is separate, so we can create usergroups where we don't wish to set permissions, i.e. we are just grouping users for organizational reasons and to reduce the length of the form if we do not need these options. The eight options available to us with this option enabled are as follows:

- Modules
- Tables (listing)
- Tables (modify)
- Page types
- Allowed excludefields
- Explicitly allow/deny field values
- Limit to language
- Custom module options

Modules

The first access permission that we can set is access to the **Modules**, which are the main areas of the back end. The contents of **Modules** are shown in the following screenshot:

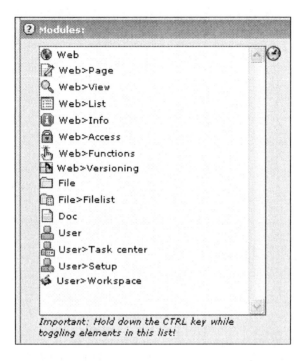

We then select the modules that we want to be available to the usergroup.

 To select more then one module, hold down the *Ctrl* key while selecting the modules from the list.

If we make a mistake and wish to undo the last changes we have made, we can click the revert selection button which is as shown:

Tables (modify)

Although the next access option is **Tables (listing)**, the modify option is more useful.
It provides some of the settings that we may need for the **Tables (listing)** section.
The contents of **Tables (modify)** are shown in the following screenshot:

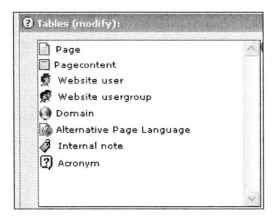

The page, page content, website user, website usergroup, domain, alternative page
languages, internal note, and acronym are stored in separate database tables. This
setting sets which of these tables we are allowed to modify. Multiple selections and
reverting selections apply here too.

Tables (listing)

The difference between this and the **Tables (modify)** option is that the modify option
restricts which table a user can change, whereas the listing option restricts which
of these a user may actually see. This section need not be set if a user has modify
permissions to all of the tables that they are required to view. The contents of **Tables
(listing)** are shown in the following screenshot:

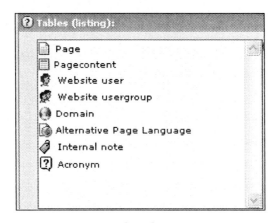

The help system for TYPO3 regards this as an unimportant option, as it is a rare situation in which we would wish for a user to be able to see but not modify these options.

Page Types

The **Page Types** options allow us to specify which type of page a user may create. If we have a group who are in charge of managing sponsors and affiliates only, we may only wish to grant them permission to create the **External URL** type of page.

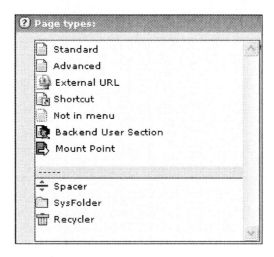

We can use the revert selection button to undo any changes, and use the *Ctrl* key to select multiple options from the list.

Allowed Excludefields

By default, some fields are not available, but we can enable these by setting them from the list of excluded fields. The list of **Allowed excludefields** is displayed in the following screenshot:

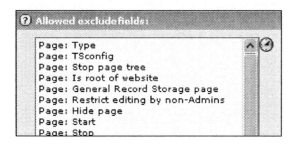

Explicitly Allow/Deny Field Values

By default, these values are something that users of this group can set, so users of any group by default can set headers, text elements, text with images, images, and so on. We can explicitly deny users from doing this, so if we do not want our group to add image elements, we can tick the **[Deny] Text w/image** and **[Deny] Image** options to prevent them from being able to add an image to the page. You can see the options in this screenshot:

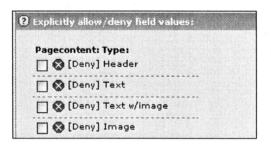

Limit to Language

TYPO3 is a multilingual content management system, which means we can add languages and create alternative page content in those languages. As a result of this, we can restrict users and groups to a particular language. This could be useful if we had a translation team; we could have a group of French translators and a group of Spanish translators. Here is the screenshot displaying **Limit to languages** option:

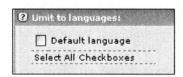

These translators would then only be able to edit the page content that is in that specific language. As we don't have any alternative language setup, we only have the **Default language** option.

Custom Module Options

For us, this section is empty! It is because this section is reserved for any permission introduced by any extension, which we may install, that wishes to utilize the permission system. Here is the screenshot:

Now we are back to the non-Access Lists settings. We have settings for **DB Mounts** and **File Mounts**. These are sections that we have not really covered previously, and mainly have uses with respect to users and groups.

DB Mounts

A DB Mount is a page in the page tree that will then act as the page root. We could set this to be our Home Page for some users, who are working on the main website, whereas users that we wish to work on new areas of the website can see the full page tree. It appears on screen as:

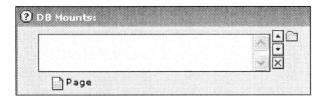

To actually select a DB Mount, we can click the folder icon next to the **DB Mounts** box and we will get a similar screen to this:

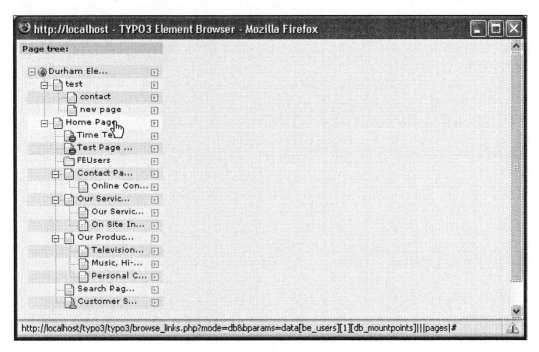

Here the pages in our page tree are listed. If we click on one of the pages, such as the products page, this page is then added as the DB Mount on the previous page (the one that caused this window to pop up). This will alter their page tree, as shown in the following screenshot:

This page tree only contains **Our Products** and all the sub-pages, while the other pages are not included because we set the Home Page as the user's DB Mount.

File Mounts

A File mount allows the user or group to access files stored in the `fileadmin` folder on our server. This could be useful if we have a marketing group that is responsible for creating pages for all of our products. We could assign a mount point that is a folder we have created on the web server that contains images and information they need to access.

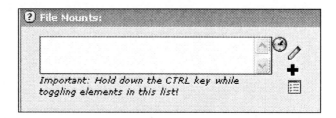

The icons on the right-hand side allow us to:

- Edit file mounts
- Add file mounts
- List file mounts

The options are shown in the following screenshot in the same order:

Workspace Permissions

A workspace allows groups of users to work together to process draft content. The **Workspace permission** are really useful options in TYPO3. They define how users of the group can edit and manage content. The options for **Workspace permissions** are shown in the following screenshot:

We have the following options:

- Edit Live
- Edit Draft
- Create new workspace projects

The **Edit Live (Online)** option will automatically apply changes that users of this group make; this permission is ideal for an editors group, whereas the **Edit Draft (Offline)** setting is ideal for users whose work needs prior approval first. We will cover workspaces in Chapter 7.

Options for Groups

If we set the **Hide in lists** option, then we will not see this usergroup in any lists that allow us to select groups. This may be useful if we have most members as part of multiple groups, one group for their permissions, and another one to reflect their staff position in the business, which other users do not need to see as the groups have no permissions or features.

We can assign permissions to a group from other groups by adding these as subgroups, using the **Sub Groups** option. We can enter a description of the group in the **Description** box, for instance if we have an editors group, we might have a description like "Editors approve content from most users before it goes online." These three options are shown in the screenshot:

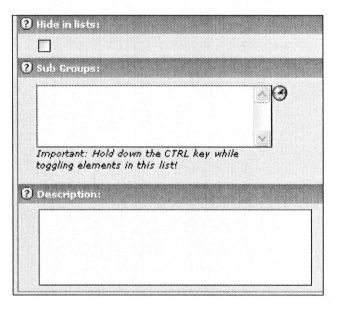

TSconfig

The final option to us is **TSconfig**. This is an advanced option that allows us to add additional permissions. We enter the configuration in the form of TypoScript, which is a configuration mechanism built into TYPO3. There are loads of options available that can be controlled by TypoScript. You can follow the following link to get documentation for it: http://typo3.org/documentation/document-library/references/doc_core_tsconfig/current/view/.

You can even refer to the book *Mastering TypoScript* by Daniel Koch (ISBN 1-904811-97-3), published by Packt Publishing.

One simple example of using this setting would be to enable the admin panel, which is displayed at the bottom of the front end (as this is disabled for regular users), by adding the following code into the box:

```
admPanel.enable = 1
```

The **TSconfig** box is shown in the screenshot:

The **TS** logo at the side of the box opens up a more interactive copy of the instructions for TypoScript; however, the online version explains more about TypoScript, its features, and its syntax.

To save the usergroup, there is the selection of close buttons to save, save and close, or just close without saving, as shown in the screenshot:

Creating Back-End Users

Now that we have created a back-end usergroup, we can create a user to go into the group. Similar to creating the back-end usergroup, we select **New** from the context menu in the file tree.

Only instead of selecting new usergroup we select a new back-end user.

User Login Details

The first three options are the user's username, password, and usergroup. The **Username** and **Password** are the only mandatory fields, as denoted by the yellow square containing an exclamation mark next to the fields. I'm going to create a user to go in my editors group. While we are going through this section, you may wish to think up appropriate values for a user of the group you created earlier, and create that user. The login details are shown in the following screenshot:

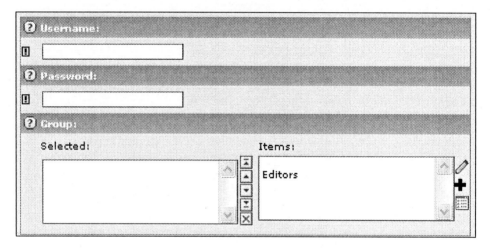

We can assign the group simply by selecting it from the **Items** list. These options will take us to another page, and we will be reminded that changes to this user will be lost if we continue to follow the link.

General Restrictions

The next three options are **Lock to domain**, **Disable IP lock for user**, and **Admin(!)**, as displayed in the screenshot:

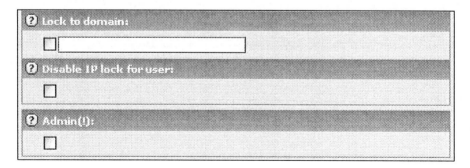

The **Lock to domain** option allows us to specify the domain to which a usergroup is restricted; this domain will be the only one that users of this group can log in through, and will be the only website they can access and edit. If we have IP lock enabled (via the install tool), then the **Disable IP lock for user** setting is useful for users who access TYPO3 via dial-up connections, otherwise this option has no effect. If a user signs in from a dial-up connection that frequently changes the user's IP address, then their login will expire as TYPO3 will assume they are someone else on another machine. This option will prevent the problem, but is less secure. Enable this option only if you believe it is necessary, for instance if you get complaints from a dial-up user who is having troubles logging into TYPO3. The **Admin** option will make the user a TYPO3 administrator, giving them *full* access to the system. Be *very* careful about using this option, it is wise to have only one admin user.

Personal Details

We now need some personal details for our user—name, email address, and default language:

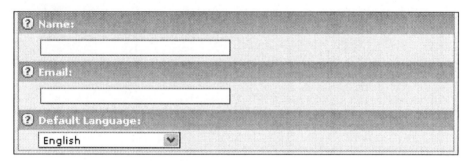

The default language setting is a nice touch. If the user only understands a language that is not the default language, we can apply it here, saving them the need to struggle to find the setting themselves when the instructions are in a foreign language to them.

Permissions

Similarly to the usergroups options, we have the module permissions. We can select the modules that we are allowing our user to access, and can undo the changes using the clock-like icon at the top of the list. Holding down *Ctrl* while selecting the options will allow us to select more than one module. The list of modules is displayed in the screenshot:

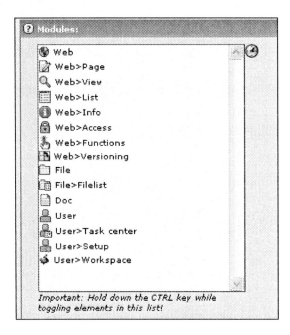

Workspaces are exactly the same as they were for usergroups.

If we wish to use the **DB Mounts** and **File Mounts** options set in the group permissions, we set these two options in the **Mount from groups** section, or we can select the mounts from the separate boxes, as shown in the screenshot:

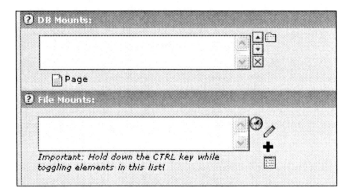

The next set of permission settings is unique to user accounts, and not settable via the usergroups. We have various file-operation permissions:

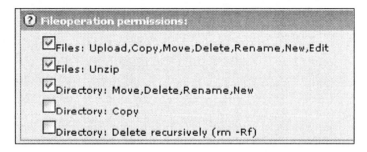

By default, users can upload, copy, move, delete, create new, edit, and unzip files, and also can move, delete, rename, and create new directories. There is also the option to copy a directory, and the option to recursively delete directories, which we looked at in the user preferences. This will allow the user to set how many levels they wish to be deleted when they delete a page or a folder.

TSconfig

Again we have the **TSconfig** option. This is an advanced option, and allows us to add additional permissions. We enter the configuration in the form of TypoScript, which is a configuration mechanism built into TYPO3. This option is the same as with user accounts.

General Options

The final options are to disable the user account, and to set start and stop times for the account, as shown in the screenshot:

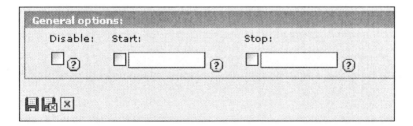

We may wish to disable an account if we are creating it in advance; we can enable it when required. The **Disable** button allows us to do just that! The **Start** and **Stop** date settings are really useful here.

Say, we have temporary staff, working over the Christmas season at our Durham Electrics store. We can create a number of accounts that start on the first of December and end on New Year's Eve (these accounts will operate only during the mentioned period). The format of the date is DD-MM-YY; so for our Christmas staff we would tick the **Start** box and set the date to 01-12-2006 and tick the **Stop** box and set the date to 31-12-2006.

Once we have completed the form, we can save it using the save button at the bottom.

Editing Back-End Users

Within the **Tools** module, we have a **User Admin** area to manage and edit our back-end users, as shown in the screenshot:

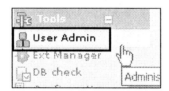

This then takes us to the **Backend User Administration** page. We have a huge list of options and these are used if we wish to compare our users. So, we can group the users by setting the **Main user group** option, and the users from each group will be listed together.

This option is shown in the screenshot:

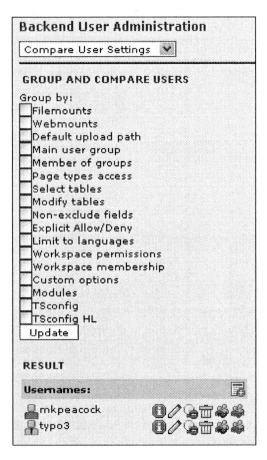

The results of the grouping of the users are listed in the **RESULT** section; by default, users are grouped alphabetically, and all users are displayed. Here is the screenshot:

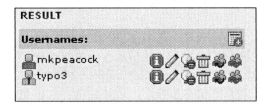

We can create a new back-end user from here too, by clicking the **New record** button that is placed on the right of the **Usernames** heading. Going from left to right, the icons next to each username are as follows:

- Show information
- Edit
- Disable
- Delete
- Switch to
- Switch back

The **Show information** button opens a new pop-up window containing useful information about the user, as shown in the screenshot:

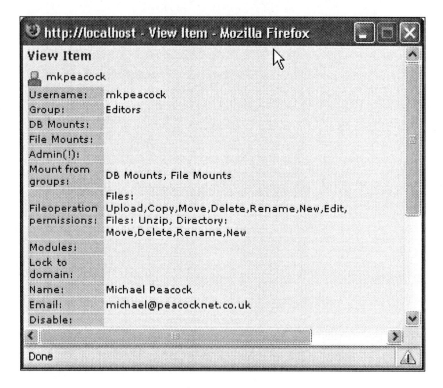

This is useful if we wish to get a quick overview of the user.

The **Edit** button takes us to the edit screen, which is a replica of the **New User** screen, except that the fields are populated with the data we have already added for this user. So, the edit section allows us to change:

- Username
- Password
- Group
- Domain lock
- IP lock
- Admin rights
- Personal details (name, email address, and language)
- Module permissions
- Language permissions
- Workspace permissions
- DB and File mounts
- Fileoperations
- TSconfig
- General options

If we disable the user, then they are no longer able to log in to TYPO3; this is an action that we can undo later. This may be useful if a member of the staff has been suspended from work, and is not permitted to alter the website during this time. If we delete users, then the only way to allow them to access TYPO3 again is to manually recreate the users.

We can see what the TYPO3 back end is like for a particular user, by *switching* to that user account (identical to user simulation mentioned earlier). We can then swap back to our original user account using the switch back button.

Editing Back-End Usergroups

The easiest way to manage and edit back-end usergroups is via the **List** view in the **Web** module.

Under the **Group** option for the user, we have the option to edit the selected group, create a new group, or list the groups. If we click the **List groups** button, we are taken to a screen that lists the groups, so we can manage and edit them easily. Here is the screenshot:

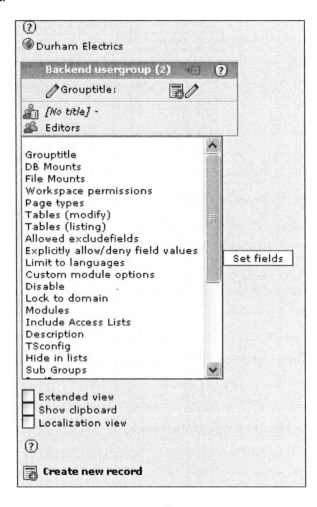

The groups are listed at the top under back-end usergroups. We can gain an overview of which groups have particular values for particular settings, by selecting some settings to compare from the list beneath the groups, and clicking **Set fields**. For instance, by selecting **Grouptitle**, **Disable,** and **Modify** options, and then clicking the **Set fields** button, the back-end usergroup table gains these fields to compare the different groups. Here is the screenshot:

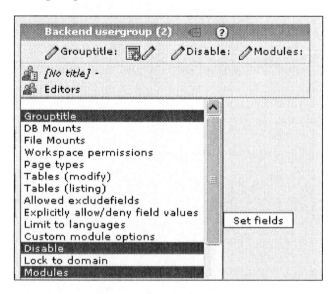

If we click on a group's icon, we get the context menu, which we often see in the page tree view:

From this menu we can create new groups, edit the group, and display information on disabling and deleting the group. Unfortunately, the edit button in this menu does not appear to work! So to edit a group's properties, we can select the properties from the list, click **Set Fields**, and then click the edit button associated with that field. Here is the screenshot displaying the result:

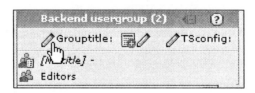

It will then allow us to edit this particular setting for all groups. Here is the screenshot displaying our back-end usergroup with specified settings:

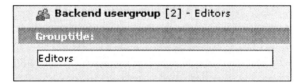

Summary

In this chapter, we have explored many of TYPO3's user management features. We have set up some usergroups with a specific role; for example, to act as content editors or as content approvers. We have created some users who are members of these groups and we have looked into how we manage these users and groups.

7
Site Administration

Now that we have our site up and running, and we have set up our users to manage the content for us, it is time to look at keeping our website running. In this chapter, we will learn:

- Why backing up is important and best practices with backups
- How to back up
- How to restore
- About workflows
- About workspaces

The Importance of Backing Up and Best Practices

All web applications and web servers have security vulnerabilities and there is every change that our website will be compromized. Most web hosts have their own backup procedures in place, but it is not uncommon for a web host to become victim to an attack, and have problems with a small percentage of its customer backups. Because of this it is very important that we keep backups of our website.

Backing Up: Best Practices

Backing up is very important. We should back up regularly and ensure we take proper precautions with our backups.

Back Up Frequency

The frequency with which a website needs backing up really depends on how often the website is updated. For a small website that is not updated very often, it should be done each week. The backups should be copied to a separate location, so that we always have two copies of a backup at any point of time. It is also recommended to archive a copy of each backup, so that if we break a section of our website later (which we do not notice for a few weeks), we can restore from an archived copy.

Backing Up Your Site

Now that we know why we need to back up our site regularly, it is time to look into actually creating a backup of our TYPO3 website.

What Needs Backing Up?

We need to back up:

- The TYPO3 files
- A copy of the database

These two things make up our TYPO3 installation. We need the database as it contains the website's content and records of the website's users. We need the TYPO3 files as they contain the website's settings in the configuration files, copies of the website's design, and copies of data that has been cached by TYPO3.

Backing Up the TYPO3 Files

Depending on the operating system we are using, there are a number of different ways in which we can back up the files from TYPO3. Under this section, we will look into backing up the files on Windows and on Linux. This is because we looked at the Windows Installer for setting up a local copy of TYPO3, and Linux is the most popular hosting environment for websites.

Backing Up Our Files on Windows

In Windows, we can easily create a compressed file containing all the TYPO3 files (known as a ZIP file), using the **Windows Compressed Folder** tool, or a program such as **WinZip**.

Provided we've used the default installation path, TYPO3 will be located in the folder C:\Program Files\Typo3_4.0.2\Apache\ and the folder that we want to compress is typo3_src. We could just back up the fileadmin, typo3conf, and uploads folders. This way, should we lose our entire website, we can simply restore the whole thing instead of having to restore TYPO3 and then our extra TYPO3 files.

Now that we have a backup, we should copy it to a separate location (preferably on an external disk, or on another computer) for safe keeping.

Backing Up Our Files on Linux or Linux Hosting

We can create a complete backup of our home directory on a Linux hosting environment. This home directory contains all of our files on the hosting account. Alternatively, we can run a simple command to compress a particular folder.

If we have a web hosting account that provides us with access to the cPanel hosting control panel, we can use that to generate a backup of our entire website (except for the database—which is done separately via cPanel).

To access the backup utilities, we need to log in to cPanel, which is located at www.ourdomain.com/cpanel, and then enter our hosting account's username and password. In cPanel, we have the backup option on the main screen, as shown in the following screenshot:

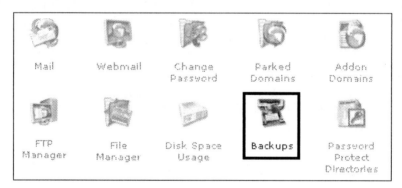

The **Backups** section has a number of options, but the one that we want is the **Download a home directory Backup**. This will generate a backup of all the files of our website and allow us to download it.

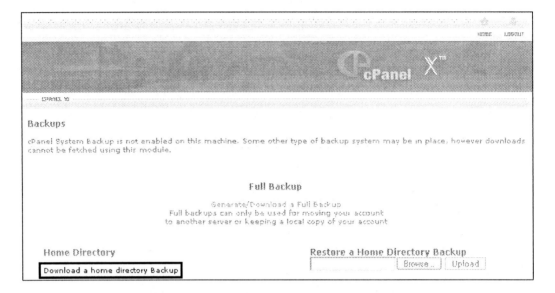

In the previous screenshot, there is a warning message. This is because my web server does not have the option to back up the entire server, just an individual user's webspace.

The backup tool then takes a moment or two of processing, and then prompts us to download the backup file.

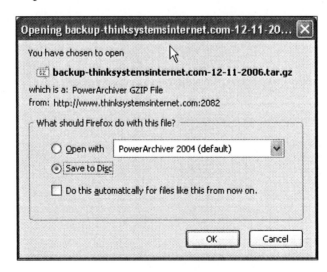

Command-Line Backup

To create a backup via the command line, we need to have SSH access to the server that is hosting our website. SSH is a protocol that allows us to remotely administer another machine using the command line.

We can use a program such as **Putty** to connect to the server. We can download Putty from `http://www.chiark.greenend.org.uk/~sgtatham/putty/`. Putty only needs to be downloaded, after which it can be run straight away, and does not require to be installed.

When we open the program, we are presented with a screen similar to the one shown in the following screenshot. We enter the server's address (i.e. the web address) into the **Host Name** box and then click on **Open**.

Putty will then try to connect to the server, and will prompt us to enter our username and password, as shown in the following screenshot:

Once we are connected, we can type two commands to back up our site. The first is to navigate to the folder that contains our TYPO3 installation. This depends entirely on the server's setup and your username, but is generally /home/*the first 8 characters of your web address*/public_html (you should contact your web host for more information or if you need help).

Once we are in the correct folder, we can use the tar command to compress our TYPO3 folder to a single file named TYPO3.

```
cd /home/michaelp/public_html/

tar cvzf file.tar.gz typo3
```

Now that we have our backup created, we can download it from www.ourwebaddress.com/file.tar.gz (where we will be prompted to save the file). We should then delete this from our server once we have downloaded it.

Backing Up the Database

There are three simple ways to back up the database. We can either use the web-based interface, **phpMyAdmin**, or if we do not have phpMyAdmin and are using a Linux hosting environment, we can run a simple command to export the database to a file that we can download. The final option is to use the cPanel database backup tool on a Linux hosting platform.

Using phpMyAdmin

phpMyAdmin is something that comes installed with the TYPO3 Winstaller and is installed on most hosting environments. The installation provided by the TYPO3 Winstaller is located at http://localhost/phpMyAdmin/.

From here, we can select the database that we want to back up from the left-hand side drop-down list, and then select the **Export** option.

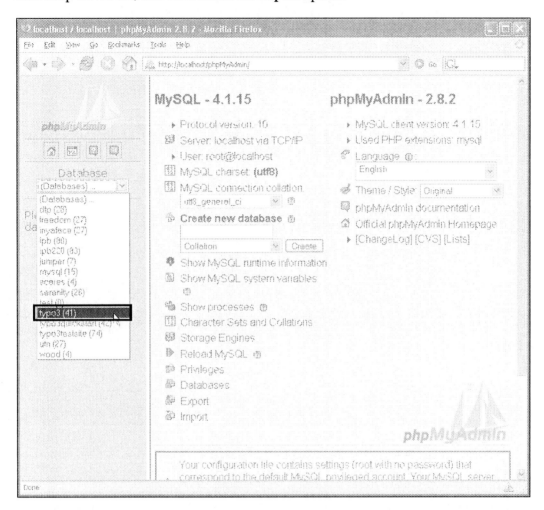

We are then taken to a screen that details the structure of the database, and gives us a number of options at the top of the page (as shown in the following screenshot).

We want the **Export** option, as we are going to export the database to a file.

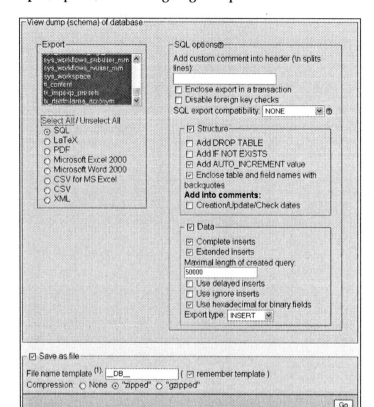

From the **Export** window, we can select the tables we wish to export. We should select all of them, and then select the **Save as file** option, and then either the **zipped** or **gzipped** option to save disk space, before pressing the **Go** button, which will then prompt us to download the database export file. The rest of the options should be left at their default values. If we are going to create a backup that we want to restore on top of an existing installation, we should use the **Add DROP TABLE** option (to remove the existing information from the database).

We can then save the file, and store it in a secure location, preferably on an external drive, or on a separate machine.

Using Simple Commands

Again using Putty, we can use some simple commands to export the database to a file. Once we have logged in to the server using Putty, we can use the following command:

```
mysqldump -u username -p databasename > /home/michaelp/public_html/
backup.sql
```

We need to replace `username` with the MySQL username and `databasename` with the name of the database. Once we have entered the command and hit the *Enter* key, we will be prompted for our MySQL password.

The command takes the database and exports it to the file `backup.sql` in the `public_html` folder, so we can then download the file from `http://www.ourdomain.com/backup.sql`. Again, once we have downloaded this backup file we should delete it from the server.

Using the cPanel Utility

To access the backup utilities, we need to log in to cPanel, which is located at `www.ourdomain.com/cpanel`, and then enter our hosting account's username and password. From here, we have the backup option on the main screen.

The **Backups** section has a number of options. The one that we want is **Download a MySQL Database Backup**. Beneath that is a list of the available databases.

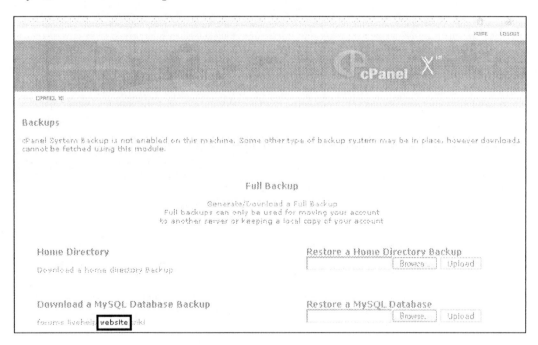

From the list, we can select the database that we want to download, and then we will be prompted to save the file at a secure location.

Restoring Your Site from a Backup

Now that we have learned how to back up our websites, we need to look into restoring them; otherwise the backups would be worthless.

Restoring the Files

There are two ways to restore your files: we can unzip them on our computer and import the home directory backup using our hosting control panel, or upload the ZIP file to our website and run a simple command to unpack the files.

Restoring the Files on Windows

We need to extract the files from our backup to our installation of TYPO3, which is at `C:\Program Files\Typo3_4.0.1\Apache\typo3`.

Restoring the Files on Linux or Linux Hosting

The easiest method for restoring our files is to restore a complete home directory backup that we have made on our hosting account.

Within the **Backups** section, we want the **Restore a Home Directory Backup** area, where we can browse for our backup file and then click on **Upload**.

This will then completely erase the content of the website, and replace it with that in the backup. It might be worth creating a backup just before we do this in case we restore the wrong thing.

The other option for restoring files on our Linux hosting environment is to upload the files to our server using **FTP** and then, using Putty (which we have discussed earlier), run a simple command to restore the files. The command is shown below, but we need to replace `file.tar` with the name of the file we have uploaded.

```
tar -xvf file.tar
```

Remember, restoring files is only half of the process; we still need to restore our database!

Restoring the Database

Similar to backing up the database, we can either use phpMyAdmin or some simple commands to restore the database.

Using phpMyAdmin

If we log in to phpMyAdmin, which we have looked at earlier, and select the database from the left-hand drop-down list, we have some options at the top. We need the **Import** option shown in the following screenshot:

This takes us to the import page, where we can browse for our backup.

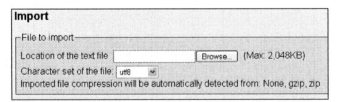

Once we have selected the backup, we can press the **Go** button. This will then upload our backup and execute the commands stored within, restoring our data.

Using Simple Commands

If phpMyAdmin is not available, we can upload the SQL file and restore it using a simple command (when logged into the server via Putty, which we have looked at earlier). The command is shown below:

```
mysql -u username -p typo3database < /home/michaelp/backup.sql
```

We need to replace `username` with our MySQL username, `typo3database` with the name of our TYPO3 database, and the present path with the correct path where we have uploaded our backup file.

Using our Hosting Control Panel

The easiest method for restoring our database is to restore a backup using the cPanel backup functions.

To access the restore utilities, we need to log in to cPanel, which is located at `www.ourdomain.com/cpanel`, and then enter our hosting account's username and password. From here, we have the backup option on the main screen, which contains the restore features as well as the backup features!

Within this section, we want the **Restore a MySQL Database** area, where we can browse for our backup file and then click on **Upload**.

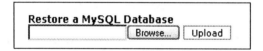

This will then upload our file and restore the backup!

Workflows

Workflows allow us to set up tasks that have reviewer users and members assigned to them. They also provide the tools for completing the tasks within the workflow itself. For example, a workflow to create new pages for new products would be assigned to an appropriate member of the staff, with their manager as the reviewer user. When the user starts the task, the **Create new page** option within the product page will automatically open.

The workflow also contains information on what should happen to the task on completion. We could set it so that once work for the workflow has been reviewed and finalized it is then transferred to a live state.

Creating a Workflow

Let us create a workflow to assign users to add more information to the **Service Center** page of our TYPO3 site.

> In this example workflow, we require two back-end user groups. The groups *Editors* and *Content Writers* have been used in this example. You should first create these groups, using Chapter 6 as a reference.

To create a new workflow, we need to go to the **New record** screen. We can do this by clicking on the globe in the **File** tree and then selecting **New** from the menu that pops up underneath.

From here we then click on **Workflow** to create a new workflow.

This will take you to the screen shown in the following screenshot:

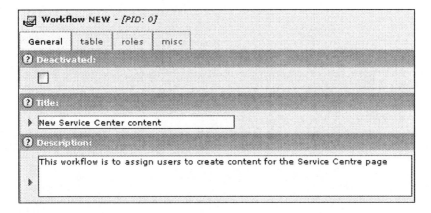

Under the **General** tab, we can select if we wish to activate or deactivate the workflow and also enter a title and a description. Note that the **Title** field is mandatory, as indicated by the yellow exclamation mark next to the field. I've entered a title to reflect the purpose of this workflow, and a description too; however, I have not checked the **Deactivated** field as we wish to use the workflow.

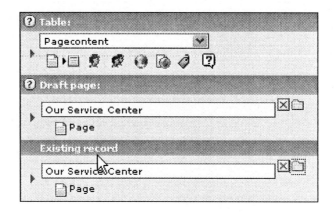

Under the **table** tab, we have the options for **Table**, **Draft page**, and **Existing record**. The **Table** list defines which type of record or content the workflow deals with; for instance, this could be either a page, page content, or even a website user. To select an option, we can either select the option from the drop-down list, or click on the appropriate icon from underneath. For our workflow, we wish for content to be added to the page, so we select **Pagecontent** from the table field.

We are going to save the draft content to the **Our Service Center** page, and then once approved, have the content appear live on the same page. We select that page by clicking on the folder icon next to the fields, and choosing the page to add it to the **Draft page** and **Existing record** options.

The **roles** tab allows us to assign groups who can assign the workflow to other users via the **To do** list section in the task center. We can also assign which groups are allowed to be assigned to this workflow and finally the review users who can review the data before it is finalized by the owner. I have selected **Editors** as the group that can assign the workflow to users, and **Content Editors** as the group who can be assigned the workflow.

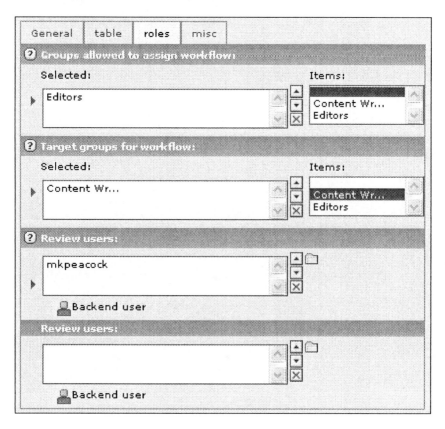

To assign the review user, we need to select them by clicking on the folder icon next to the field. If the window that pops up does not list the back-end users, we need to click on the text at the root of our page tree. This will refresh the window with the users inside it.

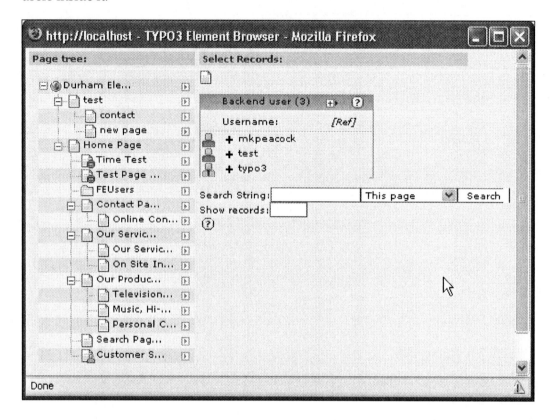

The final setting tab for workflows is the **misc** tab, which allows us to define what happens to the data once it is completed, and the permissions for that data. We wish for the content to be visible on the website, so we need to select the **Unhide when finalizing** option.

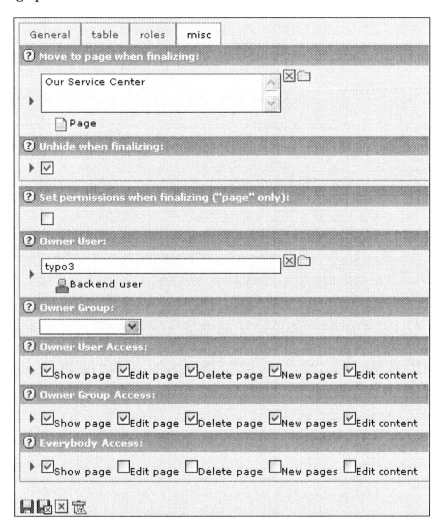

Now that we have entered all of the data, we just need to click on the save button to save the workflow.

Assigning the Workflow as a Task

Firstly, we need to be logged in as a user who has permissions to assign the workflow. Then, to create a task using a workflow, we go to the **Task center** under the **User** module.

Within the task center, we can create a new task using a workflow. Here, we can select our newly created **New Service Center content** workflow.

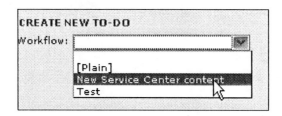

This then presents us with the **CREATE NEW TO-DO** screen to create the item. We select the user from the **Target user** list, which automatically contains only users who are a part of the *Content Writers* group. Then, we can enter a deadline. The drop-down box next to the deadline lists items such as **Today** and **Tomorrow** to automatically generate a date for us. Finally, we should enter a description and click on the **Create** button.

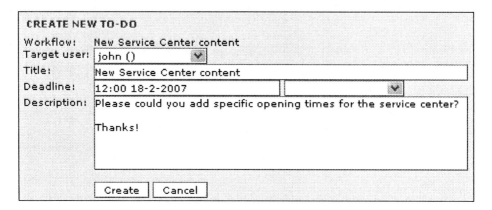

On some of these pages, you may notice some tables of system data and error messages along the lines of 'Cannot Modify Header Information'. This appears to be from a bug within TYPO3; however, the feature functions fully despite the error messages.

Completing the Task

If we now log in as the user we assigned the task to, we should see the item in our **To Do** list.

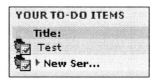

Now, if we click on the task, we are taken to the log for that task.

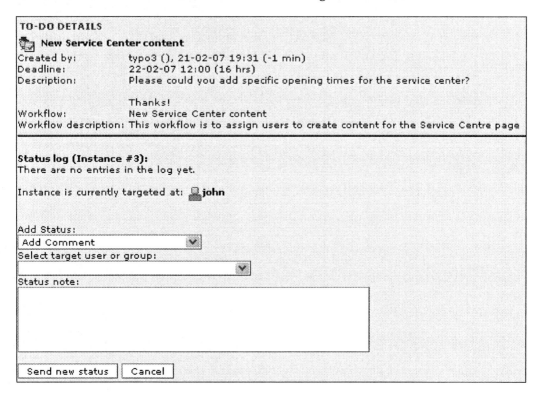

Since we are going to start work on this task, we want to apply the **Begin task now** status to it. Alternatively, we could pass it on to another user or group to do, or reject the task and not do it.

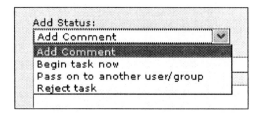

Next, we select the target user for the task, which in this case should be our reviewer.

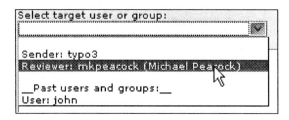

Finally, we enter a note into the **Status note** box such as a note to indicate that we are starting the task, and then click on the **Add Status** button.

Once we have selected the status and clicked on the **Add Status** button, we are taken to a page to actually create the content. This happens because the task was assigned through a workflow.

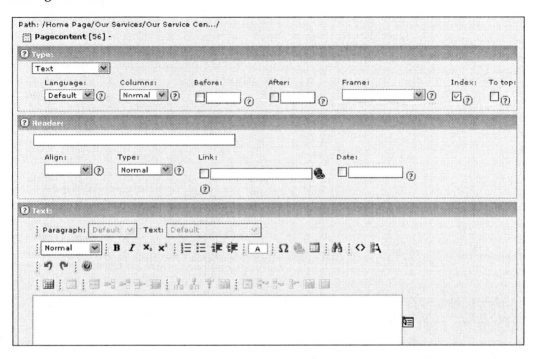

The options at the top allow us to specify the language, which column on the page we use, and even the amount of space before and after the content. We can set the header to be a link or just a normal heading, and we can display a particular date with the heading. The text options are the same as with the rich text editor.

Once we have finished the content and we have saved it, we can then set the task as complete and send it to the reviewer.

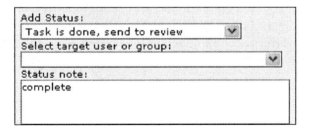

Reviewing the Task

Now that we have completed the task, let us look at reviewing it. We need to first log in as a reviewer user. Once we have had a look at the content and are happy with it, we can then approve the content.

Once I have saved the content, I am taken to the task center. As I am also the reviewer of the task, I can now assign a published status to the content and mark it as finalized, as shown in the following screenshot:

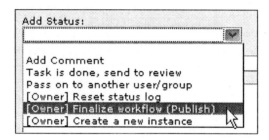

Now when we go to the **Service Center** page, we should see the content we have created.

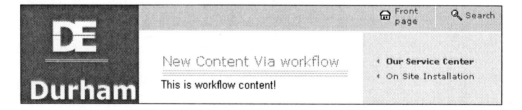

Workflow Review

As you can see, the addition of workflows to the task center allows users to assign tasks to users, and actually control the flow of the work done through this task. Without the workflow, we would only have a log, and not the physical process tied to the log. Of course, there are uses for the To Do list without using the workflow, like reminding other users of things such as meetings, events, or tasks that do not directly relate to the website.

Workspaces

A workspace allows groups of users to work together to process draft content. There is a comprehensive guide to workspaces and versioning on the TYPO3 website, `http://typo3.org/documentation/document-library/core-documentation/ doc_core_inside/current/view/3/7/`.

Here, we will take a brief look at this feature!

 Note that there is no relation between a workflow and a workspace. These are two separate things entirely; however, they can be used in tandem. For instance, we could have our workspace containing new pages that are not public, and use a workflow to allocate the tasks of adding the content to these pages.

Creating a Workspace

Let us create a development workspace, where we will keep pages for a new section meant for resellers, who are going to resell the store's stock. We will need a new page to head this section, such as 'Resellers', which is not visible to the public.

To create a new workspace, we need to go to the **New record** screen, which we can do by clicking on the globe, the file tree, and then selecting **New** from the menu that pops up underneath.

From here, we then click on **Workspace** to create a new workspace:

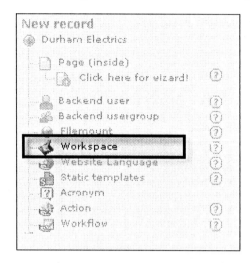

This will take you to the screen shown in the following screenshot:

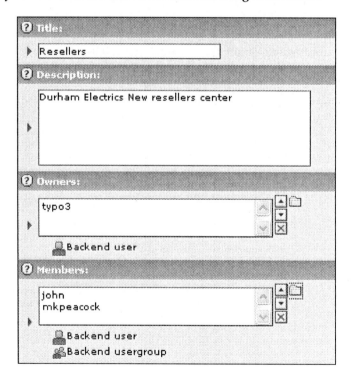

The first four options are for the **Title** (which is mandatory), a **description**, **owners**, and **members**.

Let us call our workspace **Resellers** and enter an appropriate description. The store manager, who is also the administrator, is the owner of the workspace. He has delegated the users *John* and *mkpeacock* to work on the section.

The **Owners** can add new **Members** or reviewers to the workspace, and **Members** are back-end users (or groups) who can use the workspace.

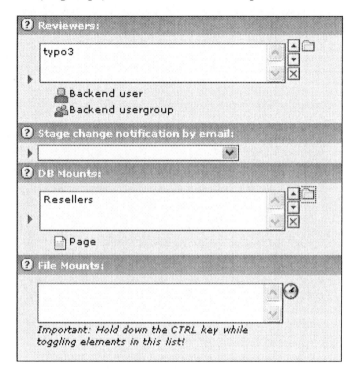

Next, we have **Reviewers, Status change notification by email, DB Mounts,** and **File Mounts.** The **Reviewers** are users or groups who are allowed to approve work from the workspace for publication. The notification setting will email members of the workspace when a user has changed some of the content from within the workspace. The database and file mounts must be accessible from the user's own personal mounts (see previous chapter); otherwise, they will not be available to them. We will set the administrator to be a reviewer, request no notification, and use a **DB mount** of the **Resellers** page.

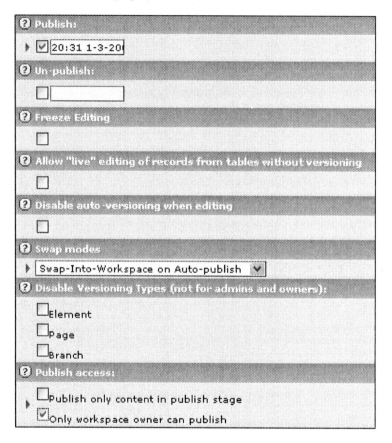

Finally, we have **Publish, Un-publish, Freeze Editing, Allow Live Editing, Disable auto-versioning when editing, Swap modes, Disable Versioning Types,** and **Publish Access.**

The **Publish** option allows us to set a time at which the content of the workspace will be published, and **Un-publish** is for a time at which the content will be un-published. For instance, if we have a workspace for a team to work on a section of the website, set up for the Christmas period, we may want to turn it on at the start of December, and turn it off in the New Year.

Freeze Editing disables editing from within the workspace, protecting its content.

The **live** editing option is for records introduced by extensions that do not support versioning. Changes to these will be made available in the front end immediately.

The **Swap mode** means that, on publication, the workspace is made live and the content that was there becomes the workspace content. We can disable the content versioning using the **Disable Versioning Types** option.

Finally, we can set how the content is published: either when the content is in the correct stage, or only if the workspace owner approves the content.

Let us set this website to go live on the first of March ready for the store's reseller programme. We do not wish to un-publish the content, and so we can leave that.

Using the Workspace

Once a workspace has been created, a user who is a member of the workspace can use the workspace by selecting it from the workspace selector in the back end.

When using the workspace, content created will have settings from the workspace applied.

Content from the configured DB mount, is the only content available in the workspace. The following screenshot shows the page tree when using the new workspace.

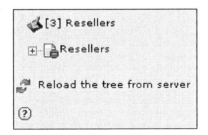

Users can be locked to workspaces too, via the user settings discussed in the previous chapter.

Summary

In this chapter, we have looked at why it is important to back up our data, and how we can back up our TYPO3 website. We have also looked at restoring the site with the help of these backups, should we ever be in a situation where we needed to do this. Finally, we looked at the workflow and workspace features and how they can be useful to us.

8
Extending TYPO3

We have our website set up, we know how to manage and edit the content, we have set up users to manage our content, and we have looked at the basics of keeping our site running. Now, it is time to look into extending our TYPO3 installation. In this chapter, we will learn:

- How the TYPO3 extension manager works
- How to use the extension manager
- About some of the extensions that we may find useful

What is the TYPO3 Extension Manager?

The TYPO3 extension manager provides a central area in which we can install or uninstall new features for our TYPO3 installation. The extension manager was added to TYPO3 to organize the TYPO3 system core. Now, features that do not make up the core system can be plugged into the system as extensions.

Extensions can be developed by third parties, leaving the core functionality to the core developers, thus allowing anyone to add features that are not available out of the box.

Accessing the Extension Manager

To access the extension manager, we just need to click on **Ext Manager** from the **Tools** menu:

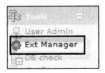

When we access the extension manager for the first time, we are presented with the translation handler. This allows us to manage the translations of labels, in the system, and from extensions. To get to the main extension manager interface, we just need to select **Install extensions** from the drop-down menu. We will cover the other options seen in this menu, throughout this chapter.

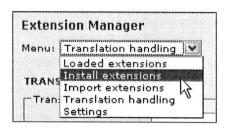

From now on, clicking on the **Ext Manager** from the main menu will automatically take us to the main interface. This will only change if we go to another area of the extension manager without returning to the main interface afterwards, as it saves the last used section.

Extension Manager Interface

The main TYPO3 extension manager interface is shown in the following screenshot, and is accessed by clicking on **Ext Manager** on the main menu.

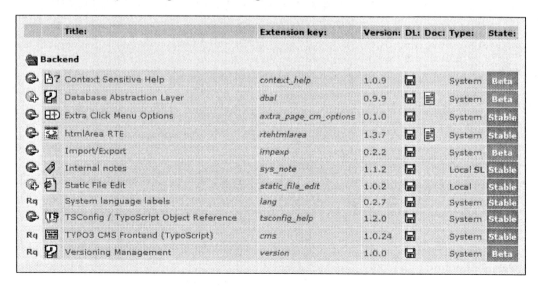

This view is grouped by the category, but we can change the grouping using the **Group by** option at the top of the page.

The **Show** options change the information displayed in the table of extensions. By default, we have the details view, which displays the following:

- Installed Status
- Icon
- Title
- Extension Key
- Version Number
- Download Link
- Documentation
- Type Name
- State

There are three different installed statuses: **Installed**, **Not Installed**, and **Required**. The installed status is a green circle with a minus symbol within; we can click on the symbol if we wish to remove the extension. The not installed status is a grey symbol with a plus sign within; we can install that particular extension by clicking on the symbol. The required symbol is the letters **Rq** in red. This symbol does not do anything as the extensions that are classed as required are required by the system and thus cannot be removed.

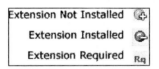

The icon displayed next to each extension is an icon representing the extension. For instance, the **Internal notes** extension has a logo of a note.

The **Title** briefly explains the extension in a few words, and the **Extension key** is a key that uniquely identifies an extension. Extension developers must register their extension keys with the TYPO3 website. For more information, see the extension key web page on the typo3.org website: `http://typo3.org/extensions/extension-keys/`.

The extension's **Version Number** allows developers to keep track of versions of their extensions; so we can ensure that we have the most recent version installed.

The **Download link (DL)** allows us to download a copy of the extension to our computer. If there is the option for us to download a particular extension, then there is the icon of a floppy disk in that column of the extensions table. If the extension has documentation associated with it, we can download that too, by clicking on the document icon.

The type of extension indicates if the extension is a **Local**, **System**, or **Global** extension. System extensions are related to the back end and its features, and local extensions are related to the front end, or back-end features that add features to the front end.

Finally, the state indicates the state of the software with regards to its development and stability. Extensions that are marked as **Stable**, have been tested and are suitable for use in a production environment; other statuses such as **Beta** indicate that the software may contain bugs and may not function correctly.

 Be careful if you decide to use an extension that is not **Stable**, as there may be some problems – so use it with caution.

Importing Downloaded Extensions

There are a lot more extensions available than are shown in the main interface. We can also download extensions from other websites and then import them into the system.

The typo3.org website has a huge repository of extensions that we can browse at `http://typo3.org/extensions/`.

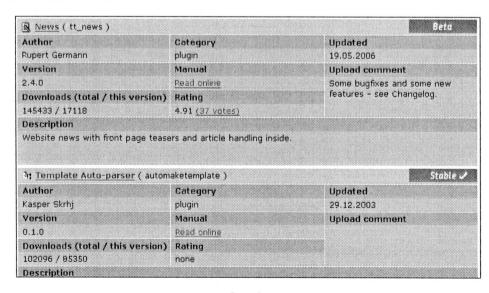

The extensions available on the website are listed in tables describing them in more detail. We can download an extension by clicking on the extension's name, and then on the following page, clicking on **Download compressed extension .T3X file**.

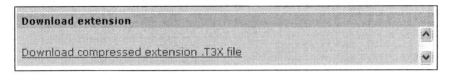

Once we have an extension downloaded, we can import it from the **Import extensions** section of the extension manager, which can be accessed from the menu at the top.

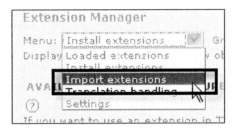

From this area, we can either look up an extension in an online repository (see further on in this chapter for details in extension manager settings), or upload a file directly to our server.

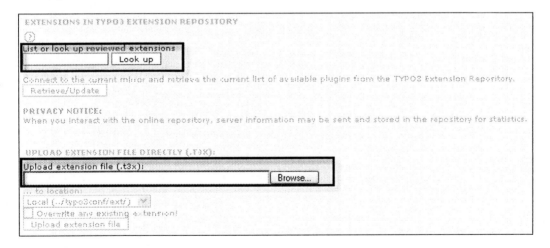

To upload an extension, we just need to select the file from our computer using the **Browse...** button and then click on the **Upload extension file** button. Once the extension has been uploaded, we will be presented with a screen informing us of the action that has been taken. If the extension is not successfully uploaded, then we will see an error message on this screen.

From this page, we also have the option to install the extension by clicking on the **Install extension** link. The extension is also added to the main extension manager interface; so we can install or remove the extension from there at a later date.

Installing an Extension

As we saw earlier, to install an extension, we just need to click on the install icon next to the extension. The extensions listed here are the ones already on our server, either by default, or ones that we have downloaded.

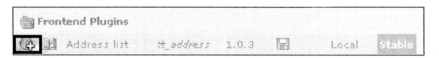

Most extensions require additional changes to be made to the database, so that the data relevant, or necessary to the extension, can be installed. Once we have clicked on the install icon, the next page displays database changes that need to be made in order for the extension to be installed. The full explanation of the changes that the extension will make is shown.

(i) Installing Address list: **DATABASE NEEDS TO BE UPDATED**

Before the extension can be installed the database needs to be updated with new tables or fields, perform:

Add tables

☑ CREATE TABLE tt_address (
   uid int(11) unsigned NOT NULL auto_increment,
   pid int(11) unsigned NOT NULL default '0',
   tstamp int(11) unsigned NOT NULL default '0',
   hidden tinyint(4) unsigned NOT NULL default '0',
   name tinytext NOT NULL,
   title varchar(40) NOT NULL default '',
   email varchar(80) NOT NULL default '',
   phone varchar(30) NOT NULL default '',
   mobile varchar(30) NOT NULL default '',
   www varchar(80) NOT NULL default '',
   address tinytext NOT NULL,
   company varchar(80) NOT NULL default '',
   city varchar(80) NOT NULL default '',
   zip varchar(20) NOT NULL default '',
   country varchar(30) NOT NULL default '',
   image tinyblob NOT NULL,
   fax varchar(30) NOT NULL default '',
   deleted tinyint(3) unsigned NOT NULL default '0',
   description text NOT NULL,
   PRIMARY KEY (uid),
   KEY parent (pid),
   KEY pid (pid,email)
   );

Clear cache

This extension requests the cache to be cleared when it is installed/removed.
Clear all cache: ☑

| Make updates |

Finally, the extension also requests us to clear the TYPO3 cache in order to function correctly. If we were to deselect the checkbox, we would have to manually clear the TYPO3 cache later. Once we have reviewed the changes the extension wishes to make, and are happy with them, clicking on the **Make updates** button will complete the extension installation.

Different extensions enable different features, some with the back end and some with the front end of the system, and are used and accessed in different ways. We will have a look at some specific extensions and how to use them, later in the chapter.

Uninstalling an Extension

To uninstall an extension, we just need to click on the icon next to the extension's name, as we saw earlier.

As was the case when installing an extension, the extension manager needs to update the database, and the following confirmation page informs us of this. If we are happy to go ahead with the un-installation, we just need to click on **Remove extension**.

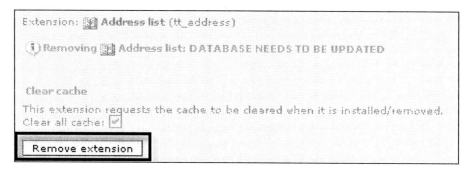

Extension Manager Settings and Repositories

Let us take a look at the extension manager's settings, and information regarding the extension repository. To get to the settings page, we need to select **Settings** from the drop-down menu at the top of the extension manager.

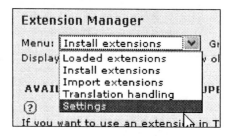

The settings page allows us to control which mirror of the extension repository we are connecting our extension manager to. When we were looking into importing extensions, there was an option to import from a repository. A repository is an online collection of extensions that TYPO3 can remotely connect to and access. The first two sections of the settings page are user and security settings.

The **Security Settings** option will allow us to enable extensions that have not been reviewed. This option is not enabled, by default, to increase security. It is advised that we leave this setting as it is.

The second section is for **User Settings**. This is used when we are uploading extensions to the repository, or if we are accessing a private repository.

The final section on the settings page is for mirrors. A mirror is a website that has a copy of the extension repository. Mirrors are used to reduce load on a central site, and to provide faster connections. The **Mirror list URL** is a web page that contains a list of mirrors, which is by default the typo3.org mirror list. Below that, we have a list of mirrors, and the default mirror is set to randomly choose among the list of mirrors. This again reduces load on a central mirror, and reduces error if one mirror is broken. If there is another repository we would like to access, we can enter it into the **Repository URL** box, to override the use of a mirror.

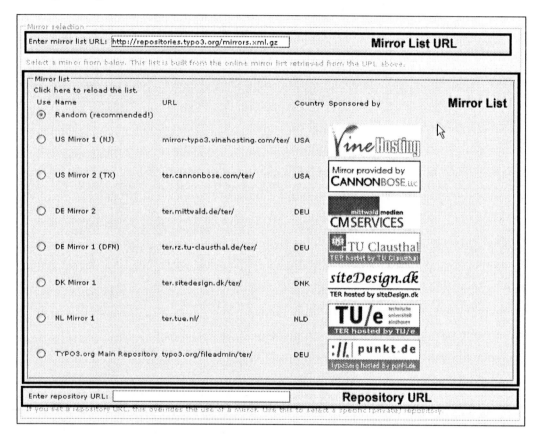

Extending Our Site

Now that we have had a look at the extension manager, let's look at how we could extend our example website for the electrical shop. As I mentioned earlier, different extensions are accessed and used in different ways; more information on individual extensions can be found in their respective documentation files. Looking at the following extensions, however, should provide you with an overview of how to use other extensions.

We will install, configure, and use the following extensions:

- Shop system
- Rating
- Message board
- Simple hit statistics

Currently, our website only provides information on products. To purchase products, a customer has to either visit a branch, or call a branch, to see if he or she can purchase by phone. However, there is an extension within TYPO3 providing **Shop-system** functionality.

To provide customers an overview of what other customers thought of a particular product or service, we could install a **Rating** extension.

A customer could tell a friend about a product; for that we could install the **Tip-A-Friend** extension.

We could even install a **Message board** to act as an online support medium for customers to communicate with staff members.

Those new features will make a much better user experience, but there are also extensions that benefit us, as TYPO3 Administrators. For instance, we could install the simple **Hit statistics** extension to have some simple statistics of page views, so that we could see which products on our website were most popular!

Shop System

Although there is a version of the shop system available for us to install with the click of a button (provided we used the Winstaller), this version is out of date. We can either download the newer version or use a different extension all together.

The extension we are going to install is called **Webformat Shop System**, and has the extension key **extendedshop**. We first need to install the extension **tt_address**, which is in the extension manager. Then, we can download the shop extension from the TYPO3 repository, `http://typo3.org/extensions/repository/view/extendedshop/2.0.3/`, and import it, as shown earlier in the chapter.

Once the import is complete, we can install it directly (from the page informing us that the import has been completed), by clicking on the install icon.

If we've used the Winstaller to install this version of TYPO3, then we may get an error telling us that the store requires an older version of PHP. The extension will still run fine; so we can safely set the option to ignore this, and try again.

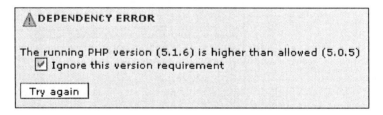

Configuring

To actually set up and use our shop system we need to:

1. Create a page to list our products
2. Create some products
3. Create a product-listing on the page
4. Create a shopping basket page
5. Change some settings

Creating Our Page and a Product

Within our products page, let's create a new page called *Buy Online*, which will list all of the products. From here, we need to click on the page's icon and select **New**, so that we can add the product to the page. If we do not add the product to the page, the page will not correctly list the products.

We then select **Webformatshop - Products** to add the new product.

We will now create a product item for a television set.

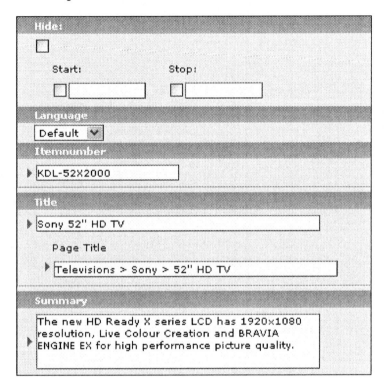

We don't want to hide the product; so we leave the **Hide** option unchecked. If this was a seasonal item, we could set when we wanted the product to be available, using the **Start** and **Stop** fields. We enter an item number in the **Itemnumber** field, a title for the product's name, and a title for the product's page itself.

We should enter a short description of the product in the **Summary** box. After that, we have a large **Description** box, where we can enter a long description of the product using the RTE (rich text editor).

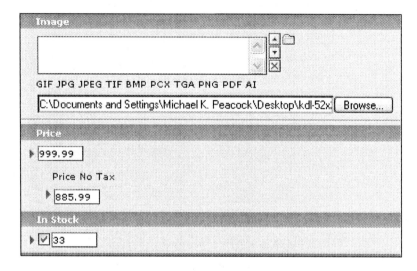

Next we can upload an image of the product, set the price before and after tax, and set if the product is in stock, and if so, how many items are in stock. The remaining options allow us to set different sizes, colors, and sale prices, useful for products such as clothing.

Creating the Product Listing

Now that we have a product for our store, we need to tell the *Buy Online* page to list all of the products linked to it. To do this, we add a new page content element. The type of content we wish to add is a **Webformat Shop System**.

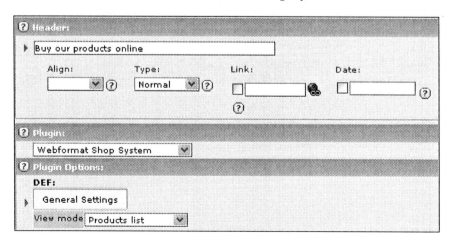

We need to enter a heading for the content. The **Plugin** section will automatically say **Webformat Shop System**, which is the plugin the content element is utilizing, and we need to set the **View mode** to **Products list** from the drop-down list.

If we now look at the *Buy Online* page, we have our product listed there.

Clicking on the product's name or ID will take us to a detailed page describing the product, providing us with the option to add the product to our (currently non-existent) shopping cart.

Creating the Shopping Basket

Firstly, we need to create a new page; so let's create a *Basket* page under our *Buy Online* page. Within this page, we add a new content element, which is of the type **Webformat Shop System** (just like the products listing page), except we set the **View mode** to **Basket**.

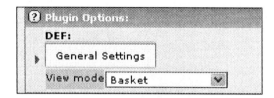

We now have a shopping basket. The only problem is that the products pages don't know that the shopping basket exists, and so, won't be able to add products to the basket. To do that, we need to change some settings.

Changing the Settings

There are two settings we need to change: the first is the ID number of the shopping basket page, and the second is how we will accept payment. For the payment, we will use **PayPal**, although there are other options available.

The *Basket* page's ID number is the ID shown in the address bar of your web browser. The address should contain ?ID=XX, this XX is the ID number.

To enter the ID number, we need to select the product page in the back end, and then click on the **Template** section in the menu, to edit the template settings for the page. From here, we need to select **Constant editor** from the drop-down list at the top right of the page. When the page reloads, we select **WEBFORMAT SHOP SYSTEM** from the **Category** drop-down list.

When the page reloads again, we need to check the box for **Pid basket**, and then click on **Update**, to reload the page. The page is then reloaded, and we enter the page's ID number in the text box that is now displayed next to the **Pid basket** option. Once we have entered this, we then click on **Update** once again.

Although this has now updated the setting, to update the pages to use the new setting, we need to then click on the **Clear all cache** link at the bottom of the template page.

The payment data is stored in a separate file. We need to open
`c:\Program Files\TYPO3_4.0.2\Apache\typo3_src\typo3conf\ext\`
`extendedshop\ext_typoscript_setup.txt`. On line 157 of this page, the PayPal
email address is set. We should change this to reflect our PayPal address.

```
#Data per paypal
50.title = Credit card with PayPal
50.bankcode = paypal
50.BICCODE = URL
50.ShopLogin = billing@thinksystemsinternet.com
50.bankname = PayPal
50.banklink = www.paypal.com
50.return = http://www.mysite.com/index.php?id=11
50.paylink = https://www.paypal.com/cgi-bin/webscr?cmd=_xclick&upload=1
```

Once we have changed this, we need to clear the cache as we did with the basket ID
setting. Once we have done that, users will be able to add products to the shopping
cart, enter their details, and click on the **Pay with Paypal** link. Orders are then
managed through the **Orders** section in the **User** module.

Rating

The rating extension available in the back end is out of date. So we need to download
this from the extension repository — the extension key is **tt_rating** — and then import
it (as shown previously) before installing it.

Adding to a Page

To add the rating functionality to a page, we need to select a page and then click on
the option to add a new content element to the page. Under the **Plugins** section, we
now have the option to add a **Rating** to the page.

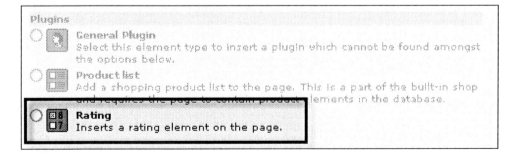

The only option that we need to change on the add content page, is the **Header**. This will be the heading for the rating section; we should call this something like *Rate this page*.

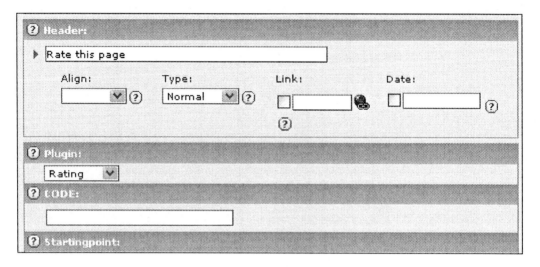

Front End

Now that we have installed and set up the rating extension for one page, we have a rating section on the page!

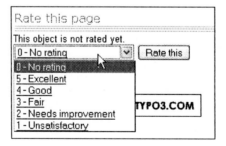

If the page has not yet been rated by someone, we have the message that the object has not been rated, and beneath that we have a drop-down list of rating options.

Message Board

The message board extension that is available in the back end is out of date. So we need to download this from the extension repository—the extension key is **tt_board**—and then import it (as shown previously), before installing it.

Adding to a Page

To add the message board to a page, we need to select a page, and then click on the option to add a new content element to the page. Under the **Plugins** section, we now have the option to add a **Message board** or **Discussion forum**. We should add one to our customer-only area for product support.

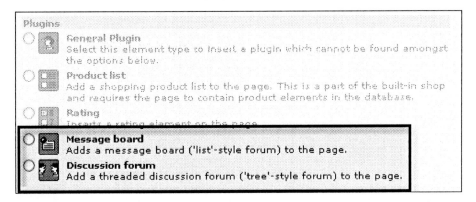

The settings on the next page are automatically populated. The only thing we need to add is a heading, such as *DE Support Forum*.

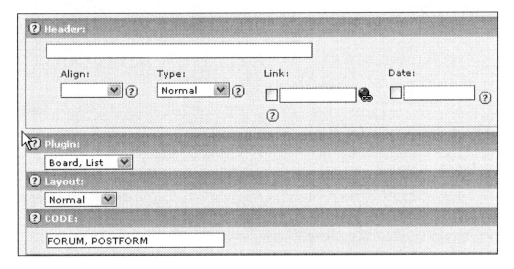

With as little work as that, we now have a working discussion forum on the page.

Front End

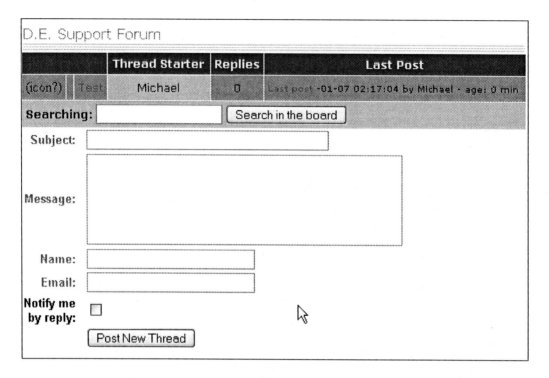

The visitor can create a topic by completing the form on the page, and either visitors or staff members can click on a particular topic and reply to a message. We could create a support page for each product, containing technical information, and a support forum.

We can manage the forum and the topics within them, from the back end. In the section where we can manage the content of a page, we have a section with details about the forum.

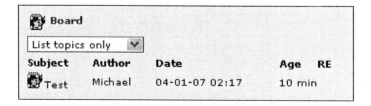

Clicking on the icon next to a topic brings up a menu, where we can chose to delete and manage forum topics.

Simple Hit Statistics

The version of this plugin that is available in the back end is out of date. So we need to download it from the extension repository — the extension key is **sys_stat** — and then import it (as shown previously) before installing it.

End Result

Now that we have installed the extension, we can access the statistics of pages from the **Info** module in the back end.

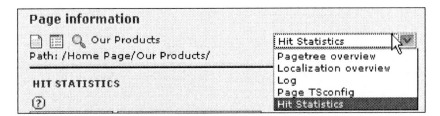

The drop-down menu on the right contains the option for the **Hit statistics**. If we select this option, we are then taken to the statistics section that lists all pages with page hits, and the time period in which they were obtained.

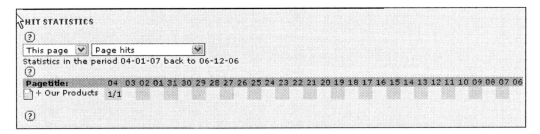

The two drop-down lists allow us to view statistics for the selected page, and various levels below that, and also change if we are viewing page hits, total hits, or hits in main sections.

Summary

We have looked in depth at the TYPO3 extension manager, and installed some extensions relevant to our website, set them up, and linked them to our site. We also know how to install and use extensions, and can enhance the features of our website easily with new powerful features.

Index

Thank you for buying
Building Websites with TYPO3

Packt Open Source Project Royalties

When we sell a book written on an Open Source project, we pay a royalty directly to that project. Therefore by purchasing Building Websites with TYPO3, Packt will have given some of the money received to the TYPO3 Association.

In the long term, we see ourselves and you—customers and readers of our books—as part of the Open Source ecosystem, providing sustainable revenue for the projects we publish on. Our aim at Packt is to establish publishing royalties as an essential part of the service and support a business model that sustains Open Source.

If you're working with an Open Source project that you would like us to publish on, and subsequently pay royalties to, please get in touch with us.

Writing for Packt

We welcome all inquiries from people who are interested in authoring. Book proposals should be sent to authors@packtpub.com. If your book idea is still at an early stage and you would like to discuss it first before writing a formal book proposal, contact us; one of our commissioning editors will get in touch with you.

We're not just looking for published authors; if you have strong technical skills but no writing experience, our experienced editors can help you develop a writing career, or simply get some additional reward for your expertise.

About Packt Publishing

Packt, pronounced 'packed', published its first book "Mastering phpMyAdmin for Effective MySQL Management" in April 2004 and subsequently continued to specialize in publishing highly focused books on specific technologies and solutions.

Our books and publications share the experiences of your fellow IT professionals in adapting and customizing today's systems, applications, and frameworks. Our solution-based books give you the knowledge and power to customize the software and technologies you're using to get the job done. Packt books are more specific and less general than the IT books you have seen in the past. Our unique business model allows us to bring you more focused information, giving you more of what you need to know, and less of what you don't.

Packt is a modern, yet unique publishing company, which focuses on producing quality, cutting-edge books for communities of developers, administrators, and newbies alike. For more information, please visit our website: www.PacktPub.com.

TYPO3: Enterprise Content Management

ISBN: 1-904811-41-8   Paperback: 595 pages

The Official TYPO3 Book, written and endorsed by the core TYPO3 Team

1. Easy-to-use introduction to TYPO3

2. Design and build content rich extranets and intranets

3. Learn how to manage content and administrate and extend TYPO3

Mastering TypoScript: TYPO3 Website, Template, and Extension Development

ISBN: 1-904811-97-3   Paperback: 400 pages

A complete guide to understanding and using TypoScript, TYPO3's powerful configuration language

1. Powerful control and customization using TypoScript

2. Covers templates, extensions, admin, interface, menus, and database control

3. You don't need to be an experienced PHP developer to use the power of TypoScript

Please visit **www.PacktPub.com** for information on our titles

Printed in the United Kingdom
by Lightning Source UK Ltd.
119552UK00001B/79